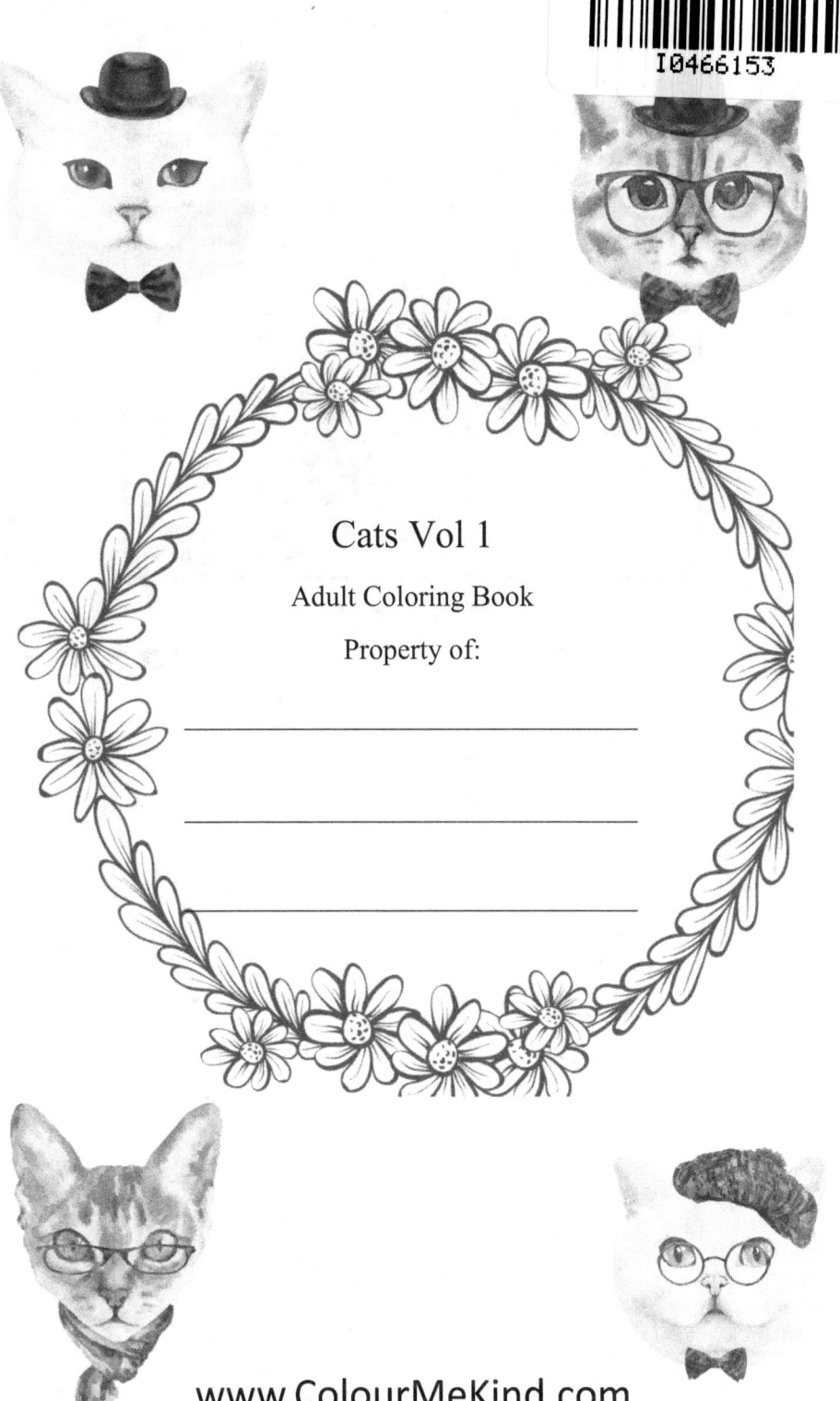

Cats Vol 1

Adult Coloring Book

Property of:

_____

_____

_____

www.ColourMeKind.com

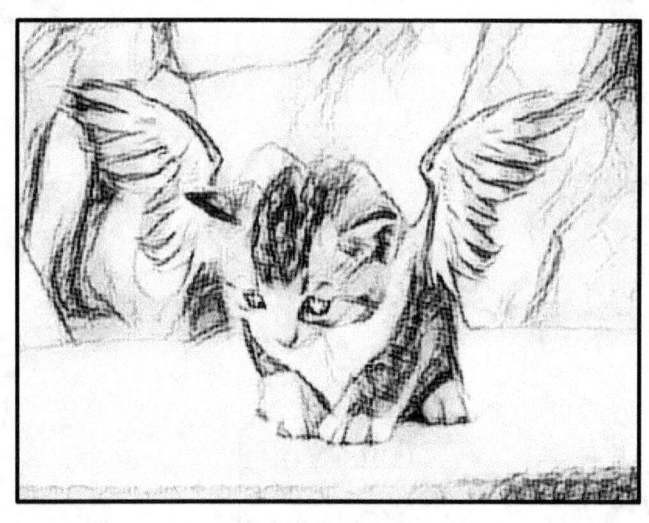

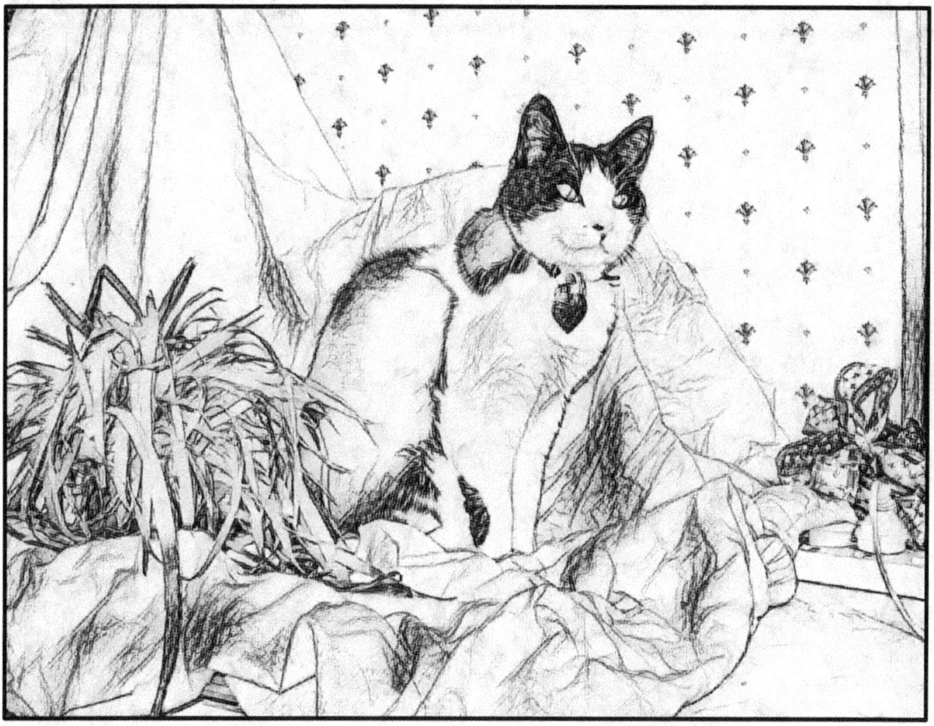

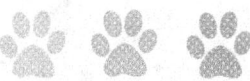

Have fun coloring in this book, because it has been lovingly filled with the pictures of gorgeous cats to delight you!

And if your colors run through the page it doesn't matter, as it just makes the inspirational thought at the back of your picture become even more multicolored fun!

www.ColourMeKind.com

In a World
WHERE YOU CAN
BE ANYTHING
Be Kind

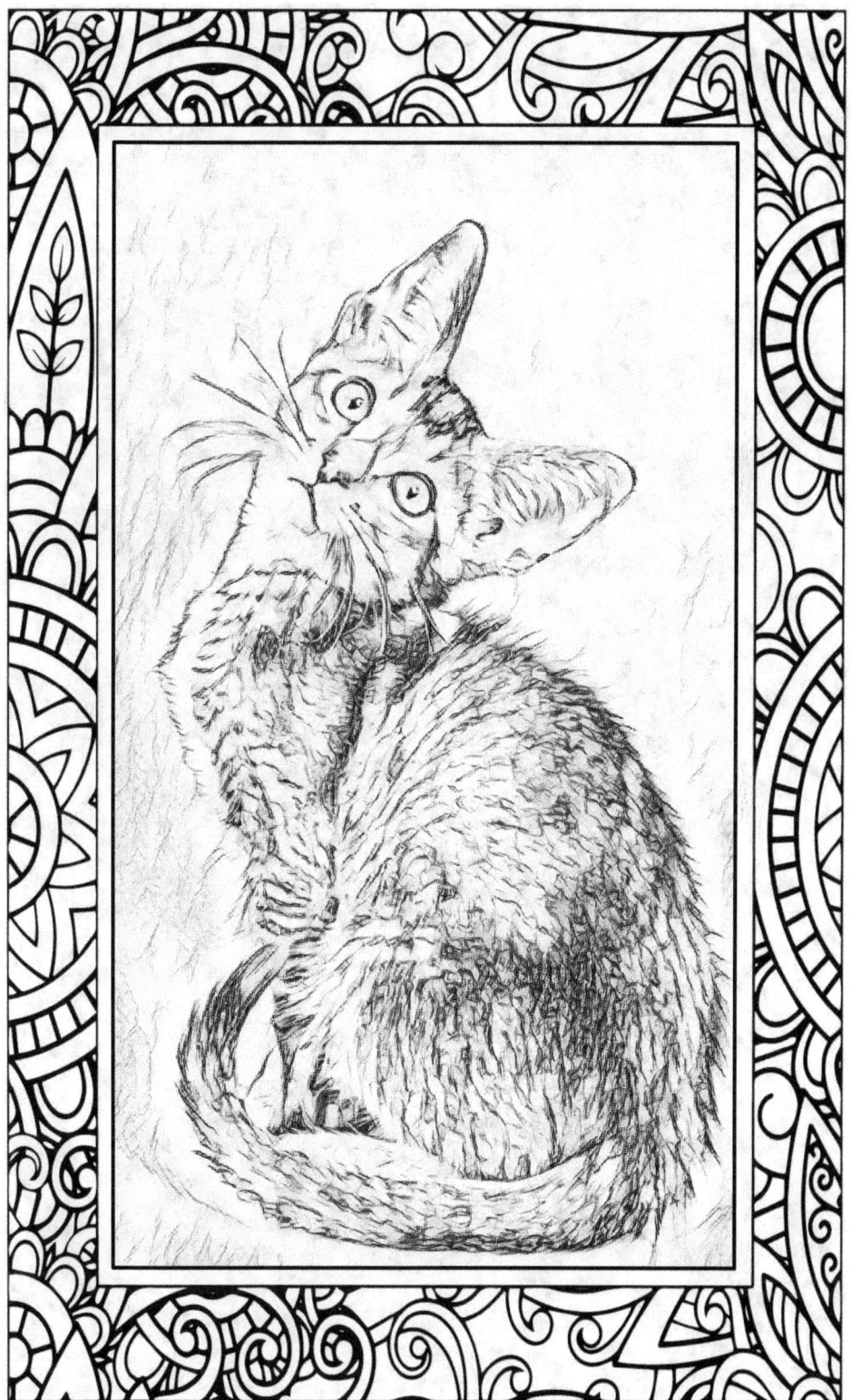

YOU DON'T
Have To Be
PERFECT
TO BE
Amazing

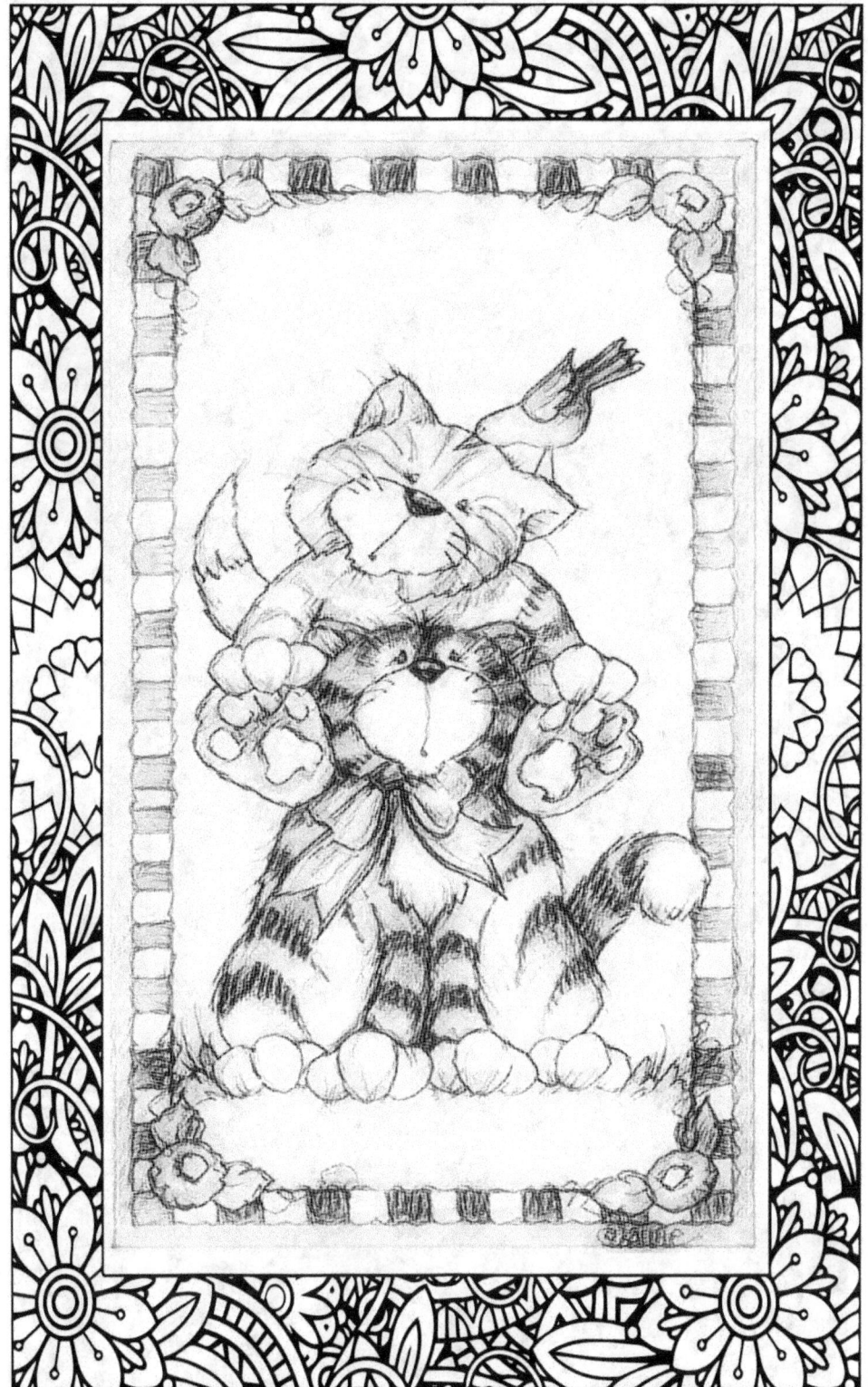

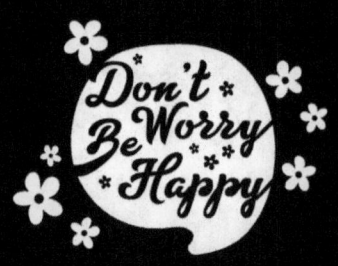

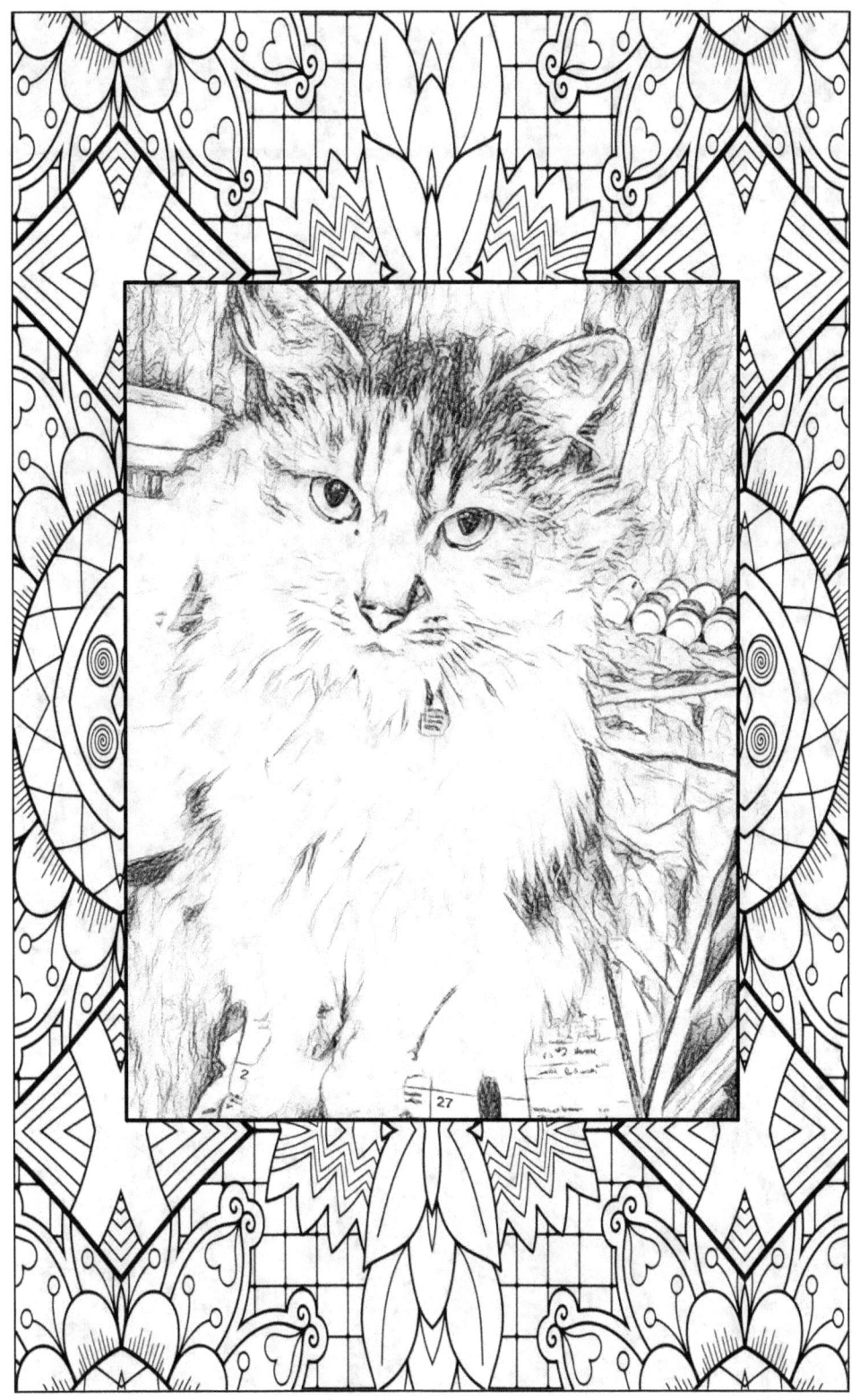

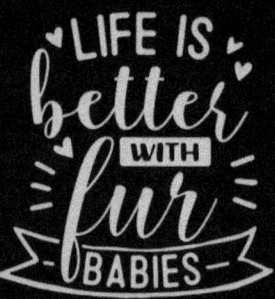

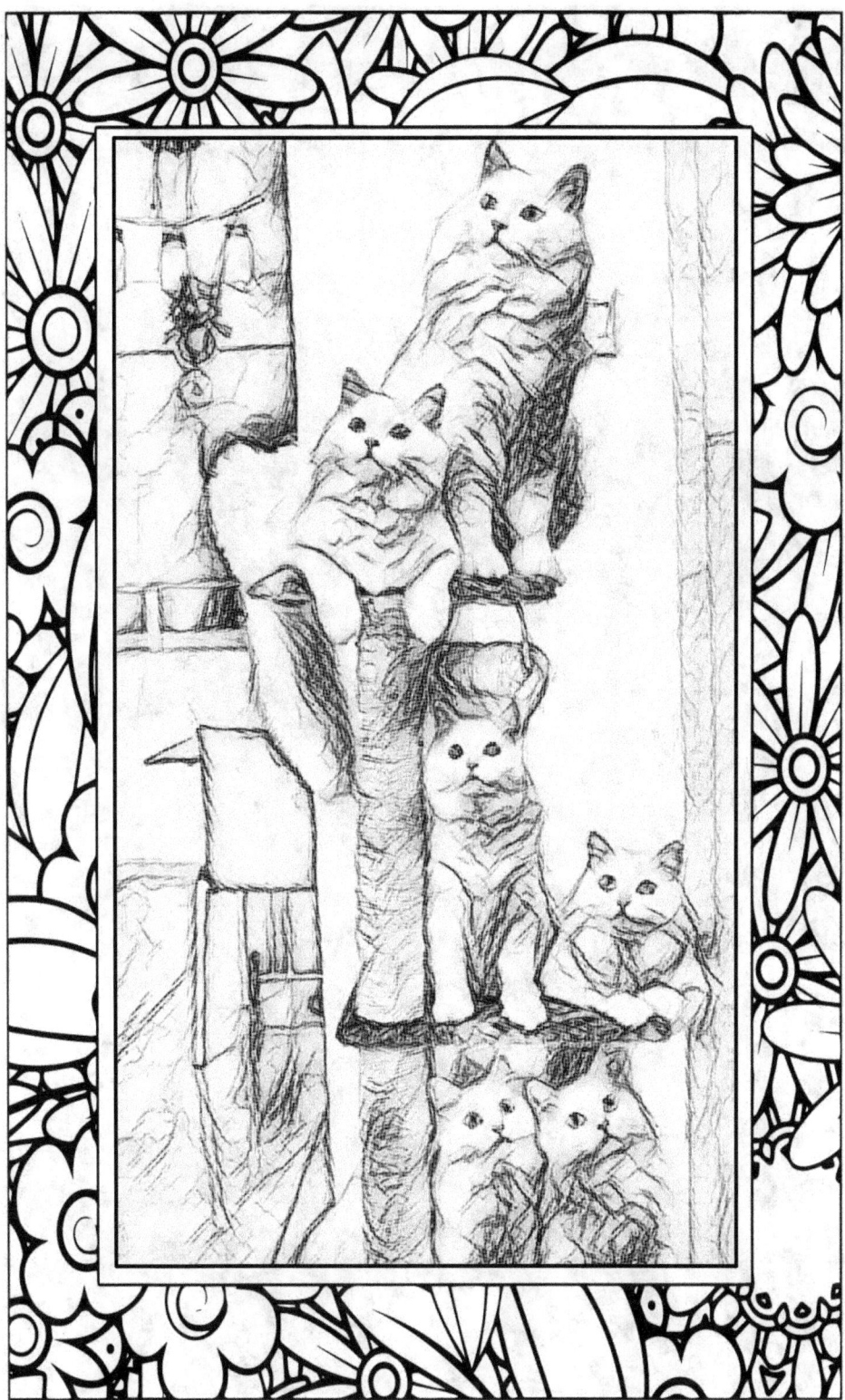

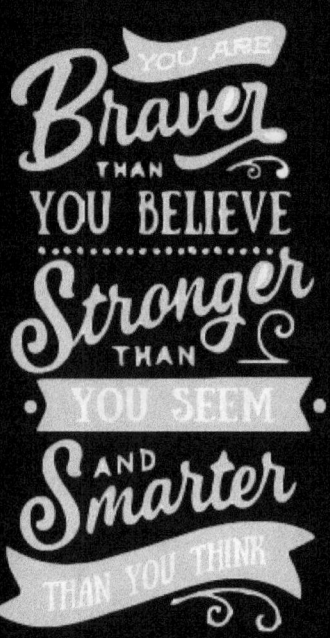

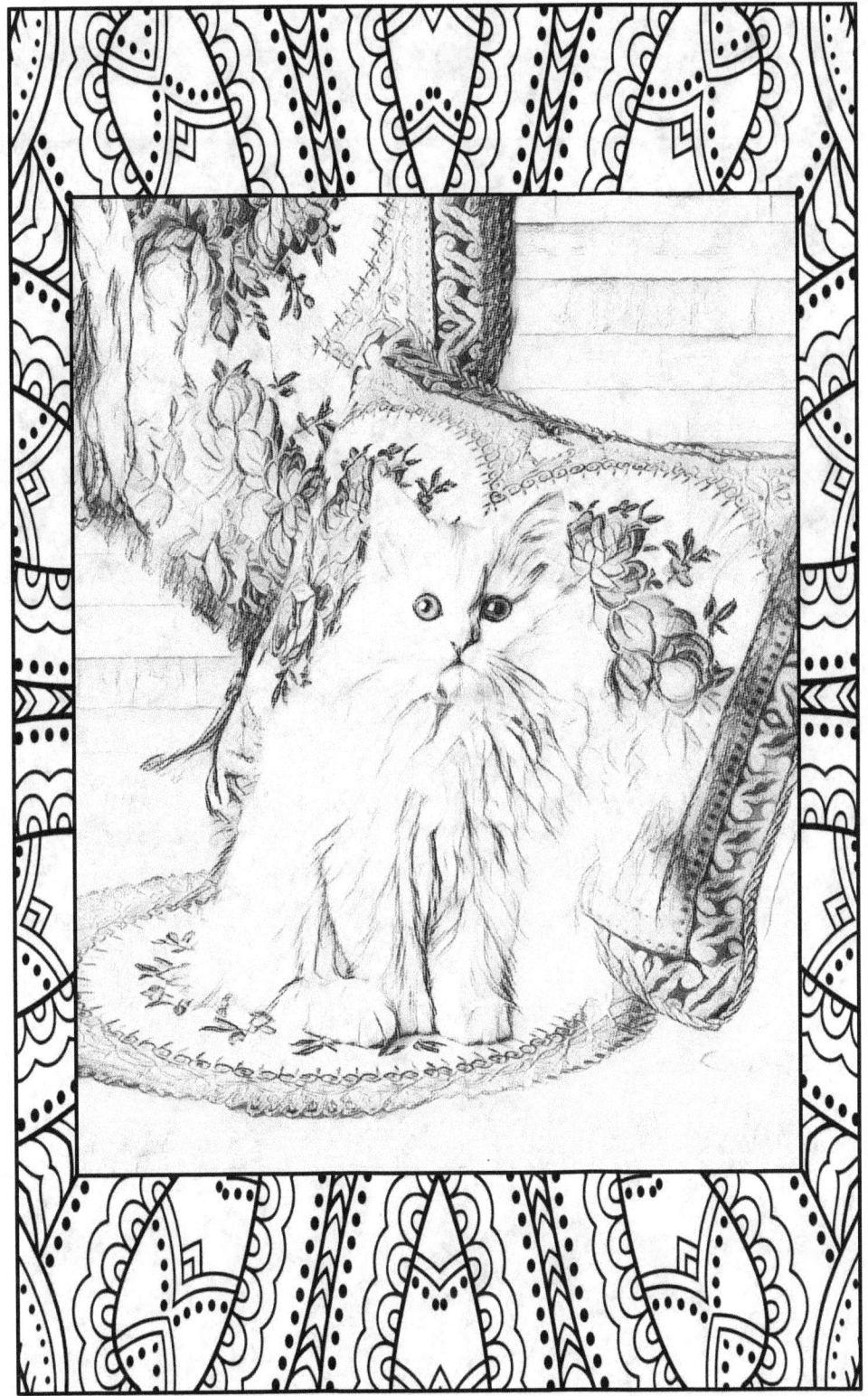

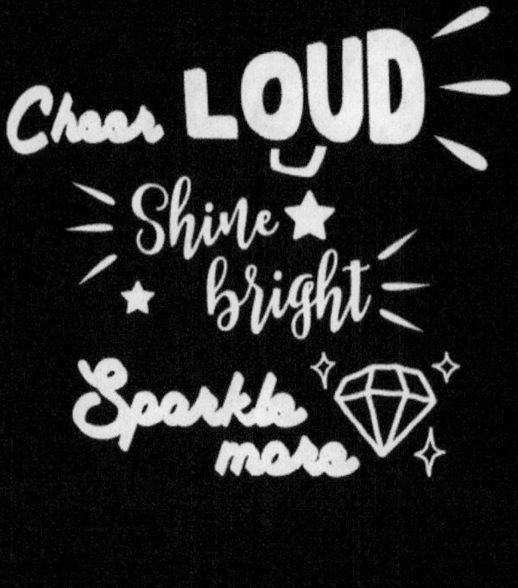

Cheer LOUD
Shine ★ bright
★ Sparkle more

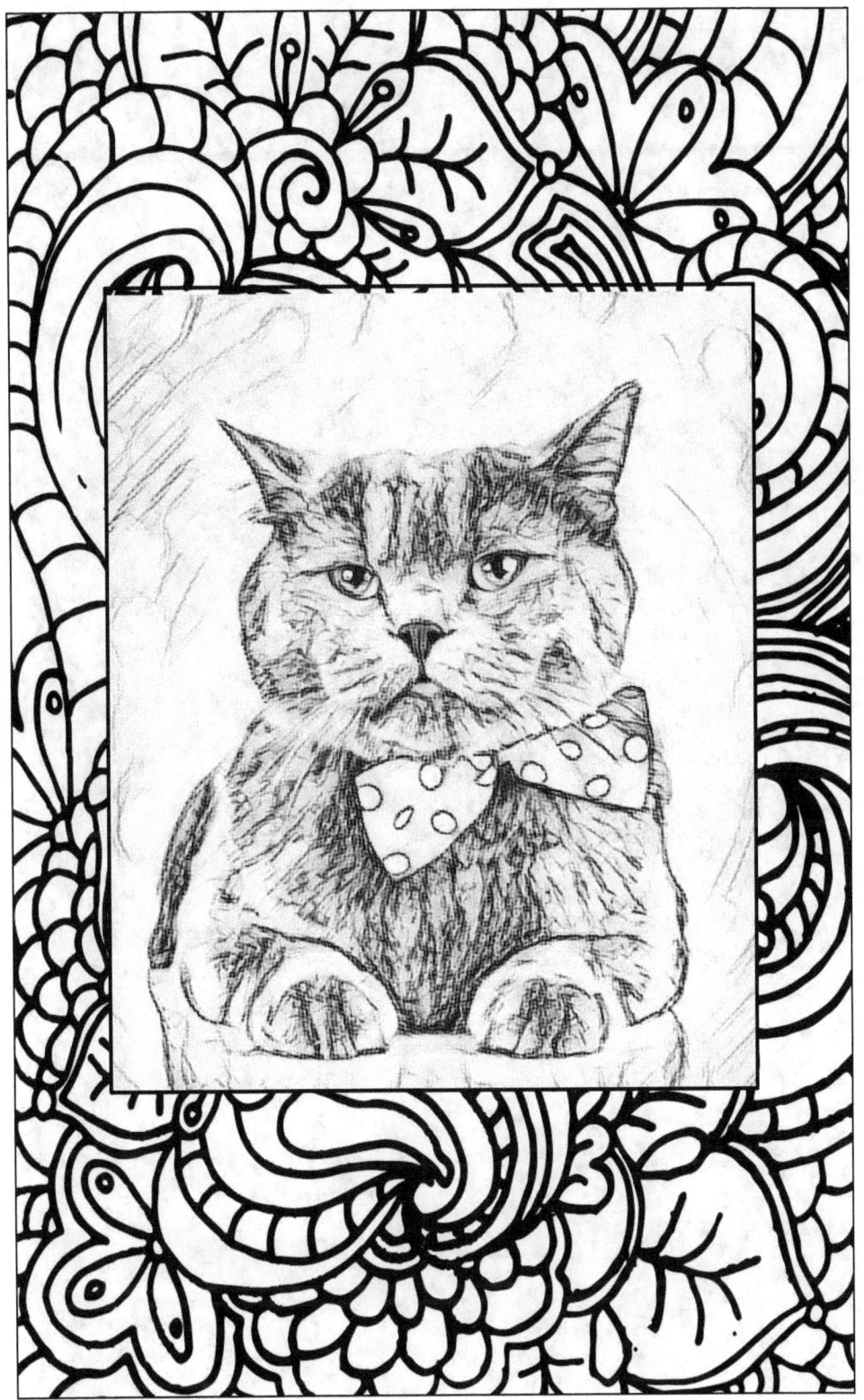

Do More
OF WHAT
makes you
★★ HAPPY ★★

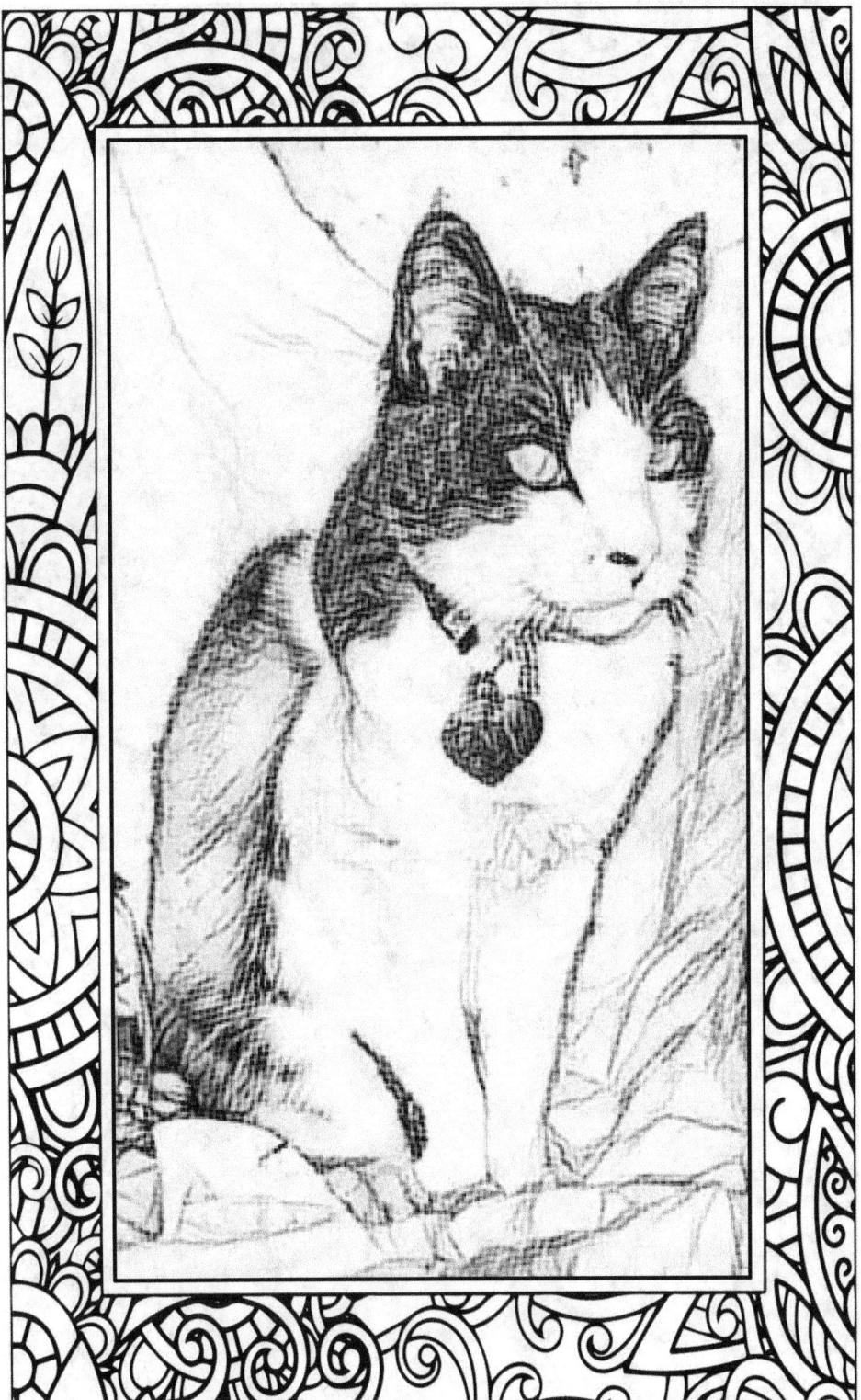

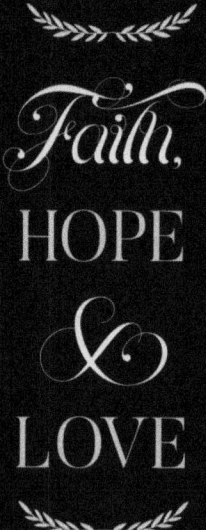

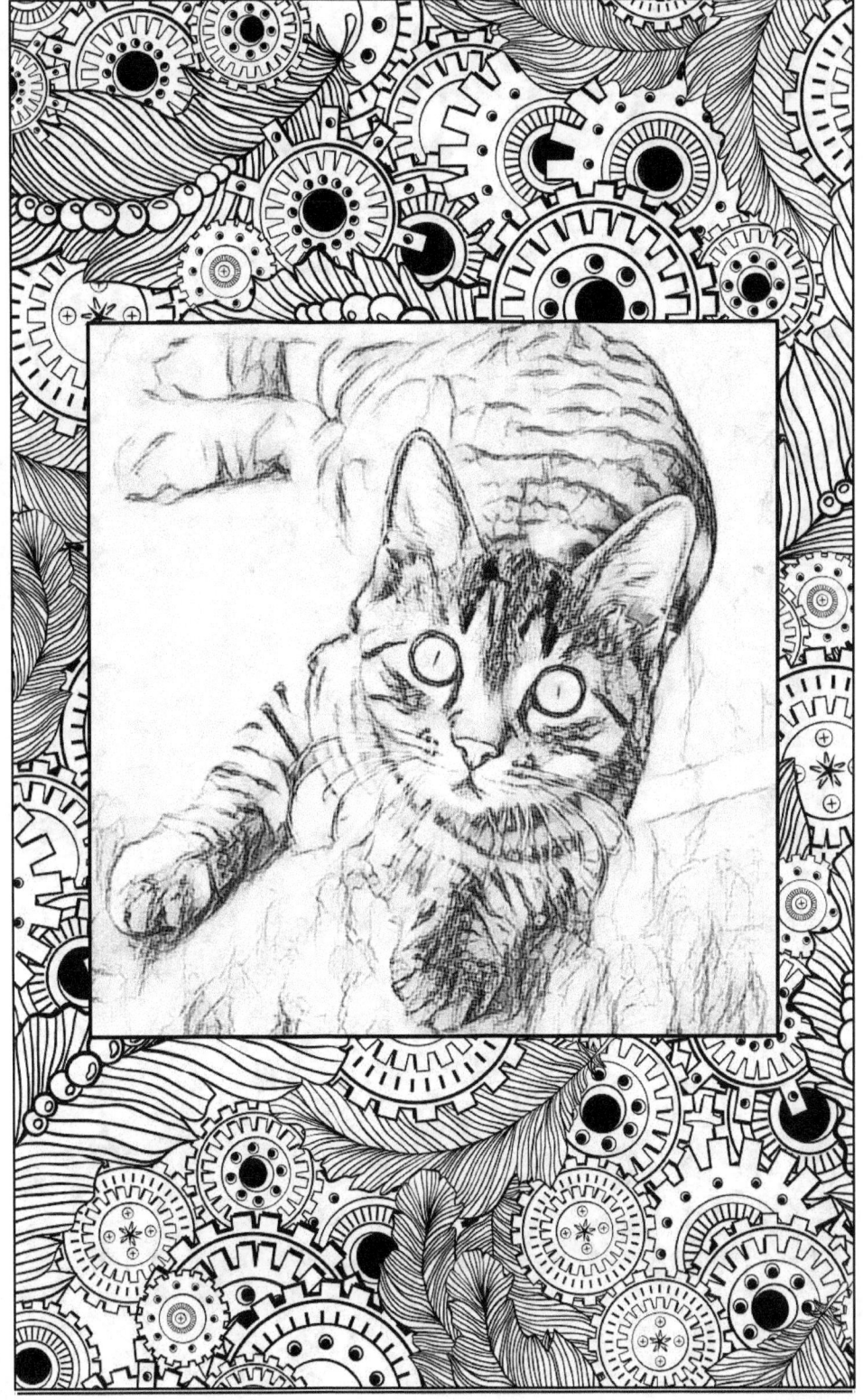

PLEASE DO NOT LEAVE *Drinks* UNATTENDED

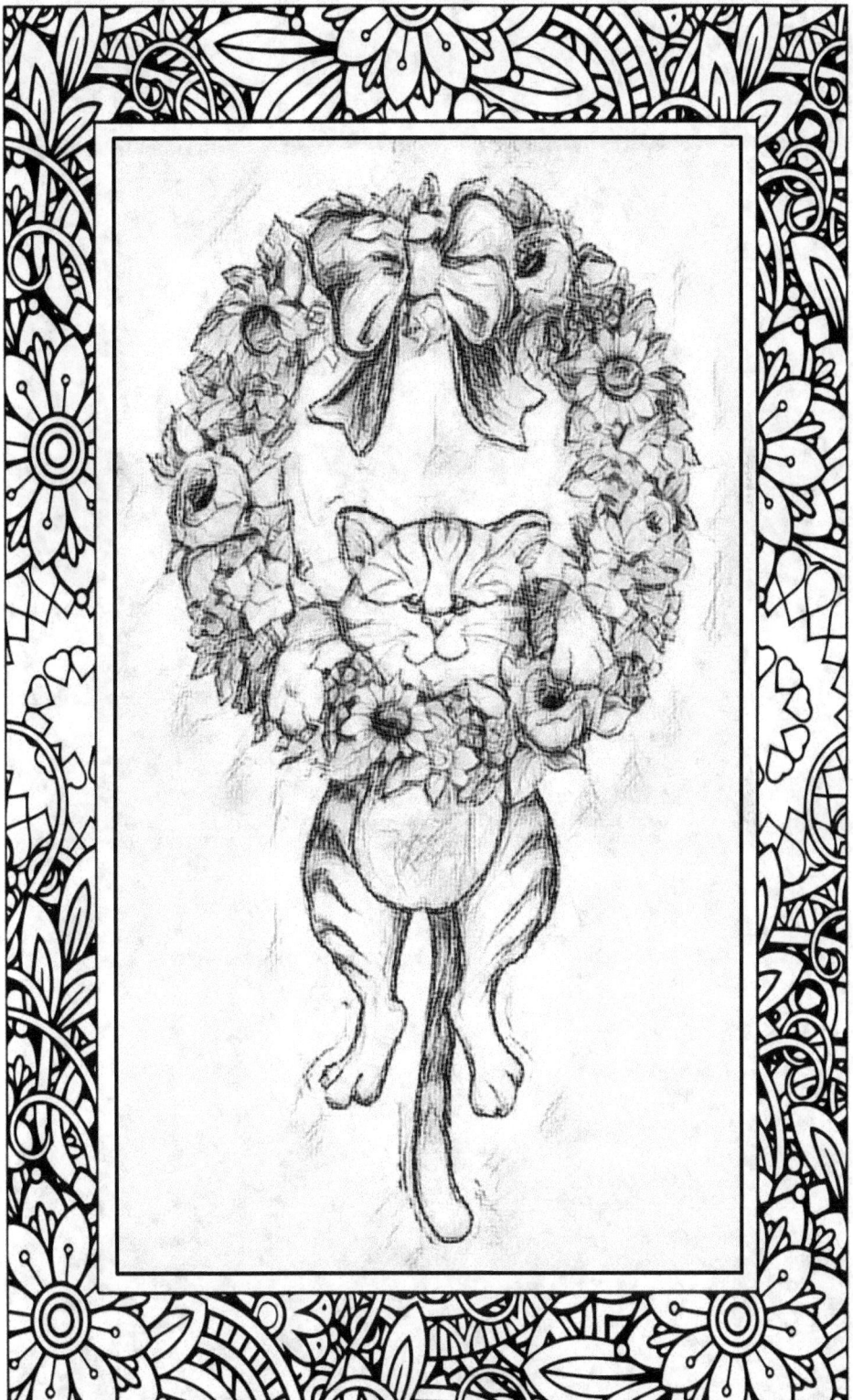

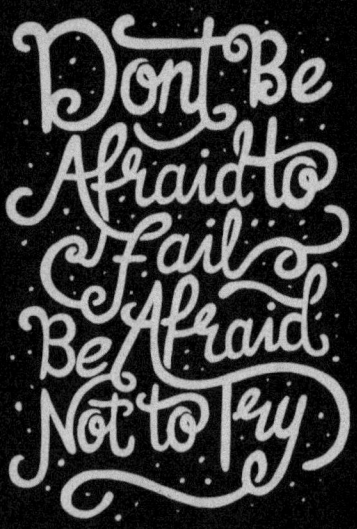

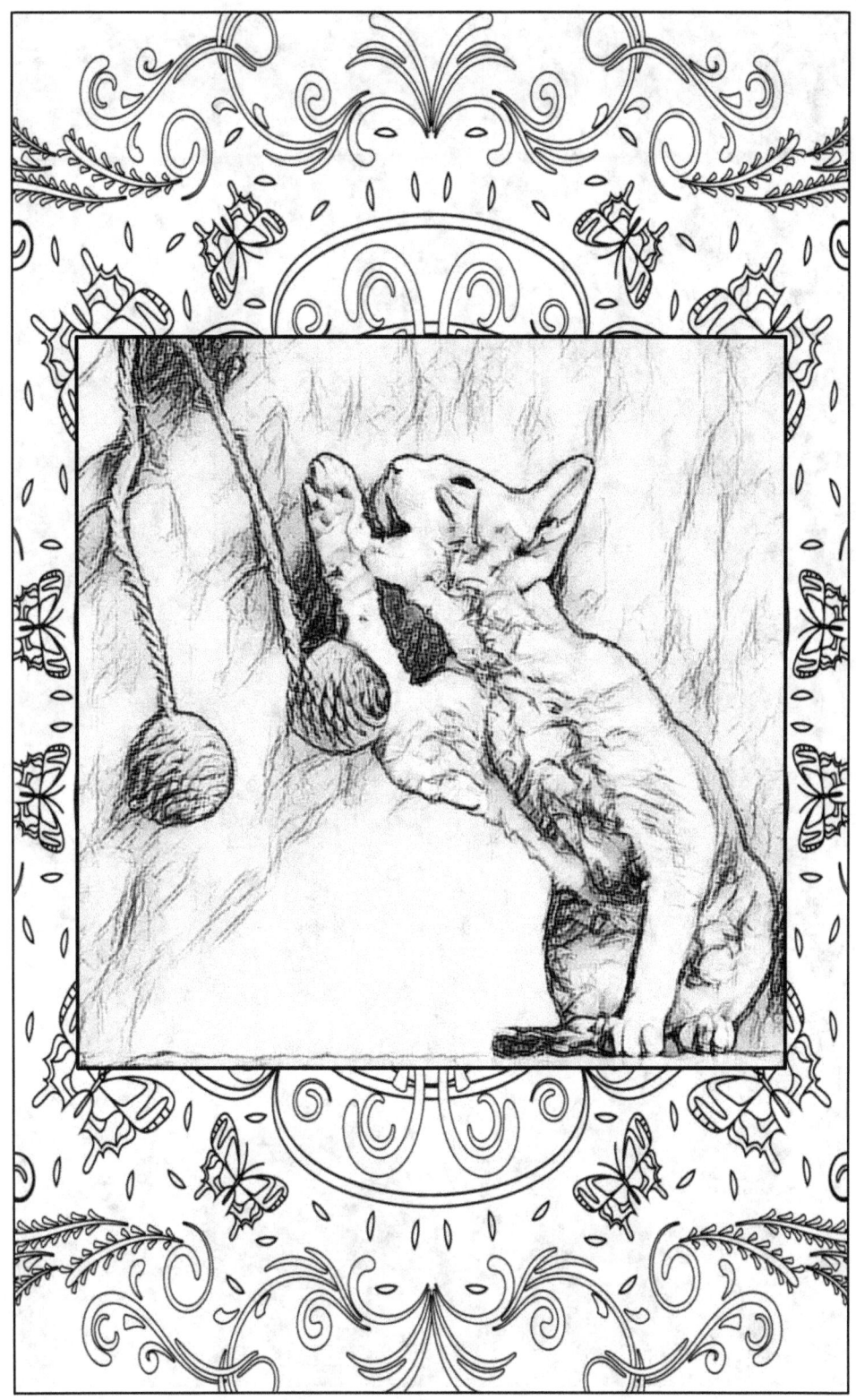

YOUR vibe Attracts your tribe

HOME

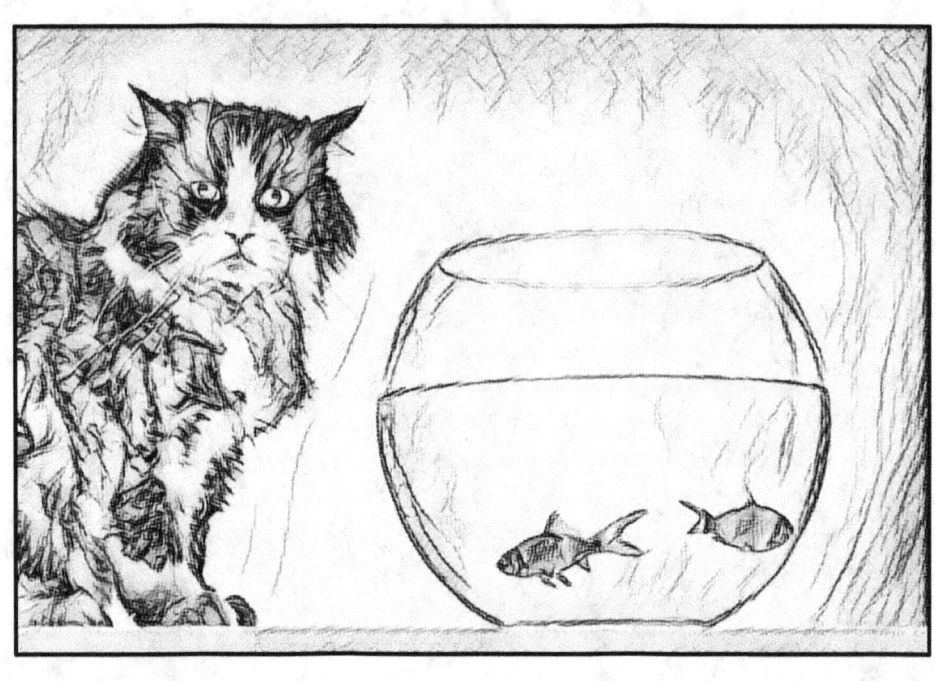

IS WHEREVER

my cat is

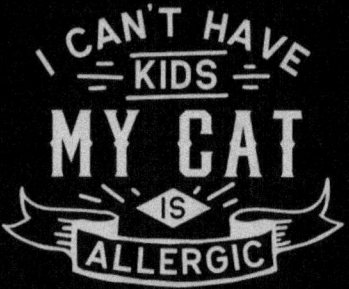

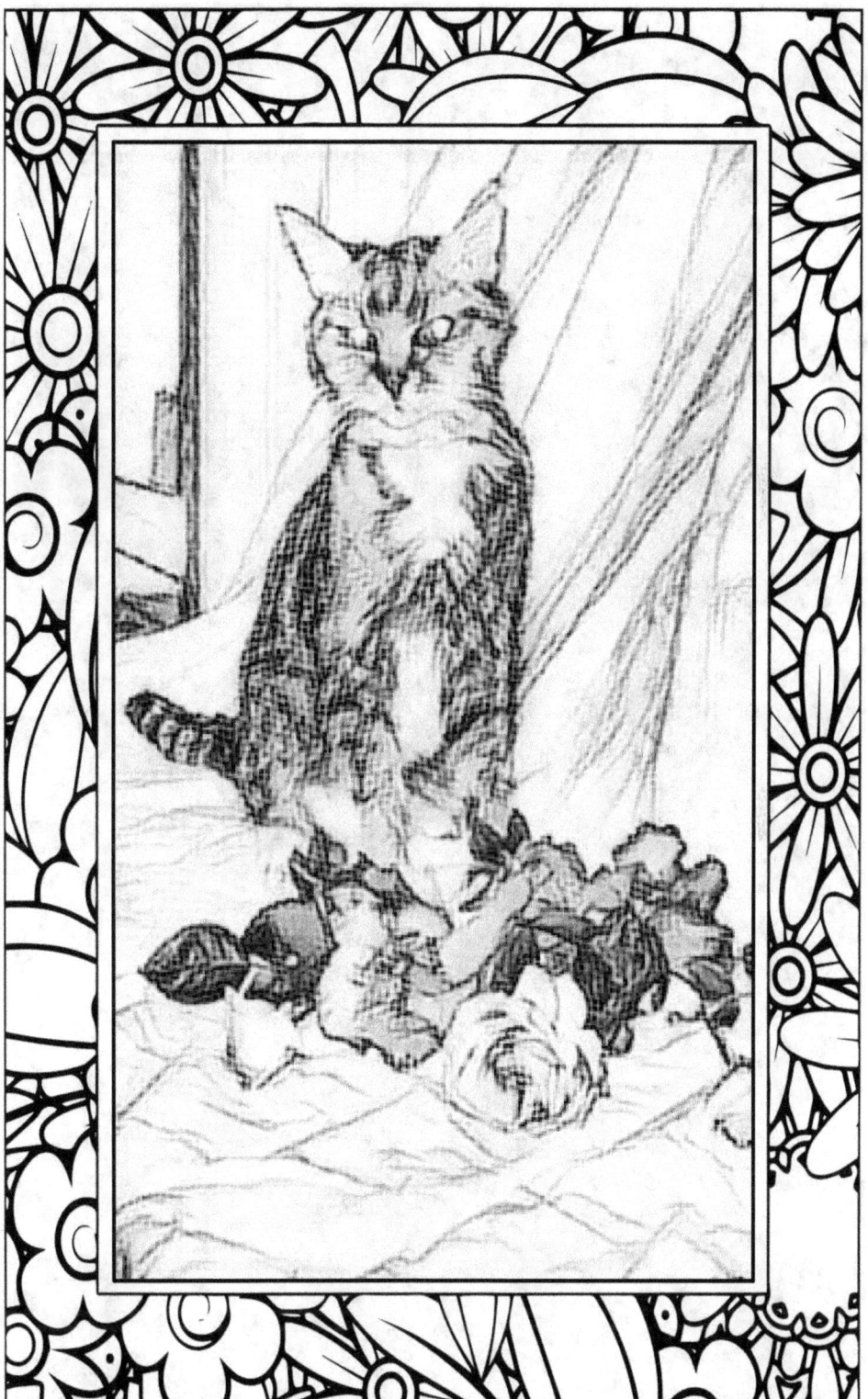

YOU'RE
PURRRRR
...FECT...

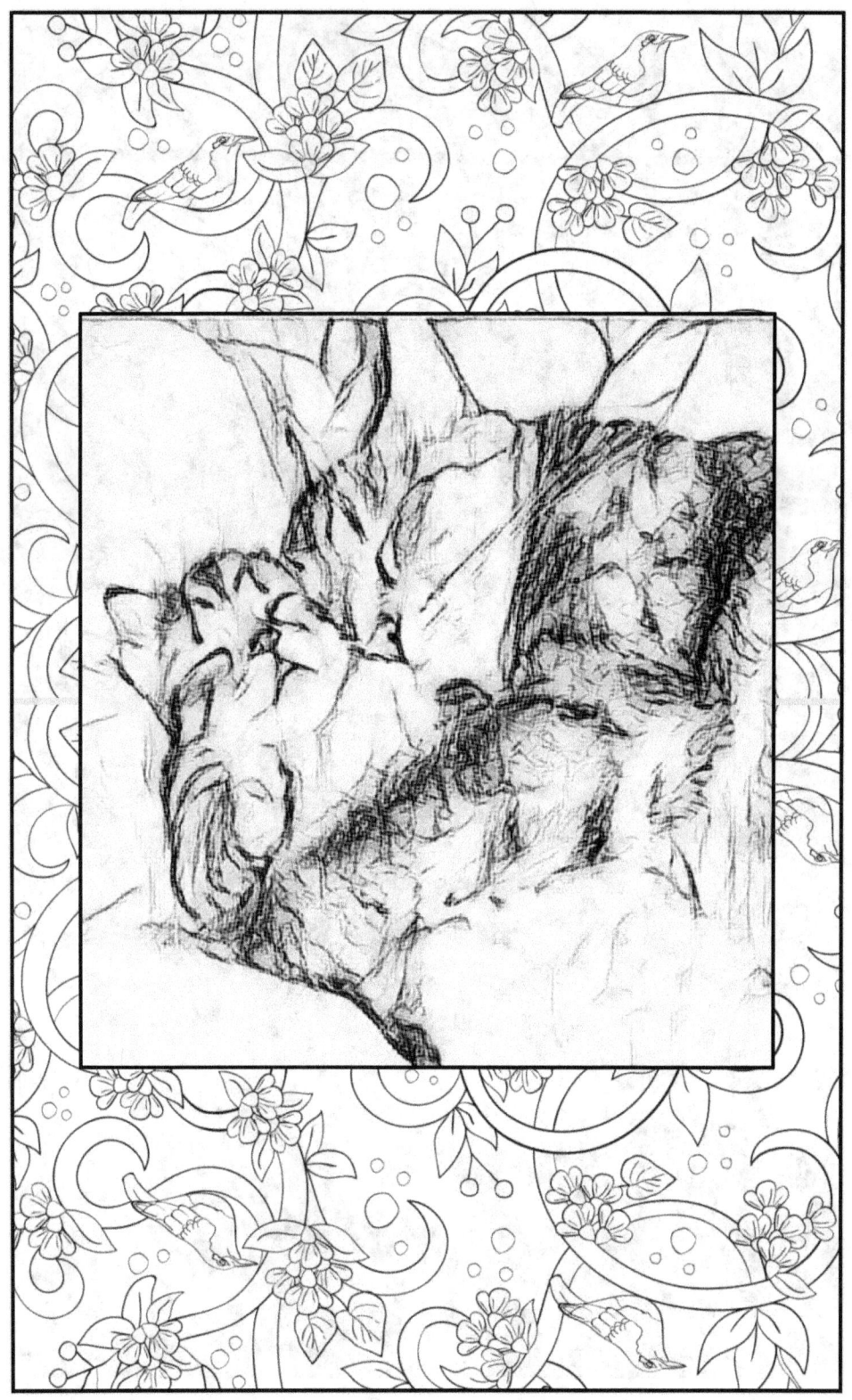

Cat hair
DON'T
C🐾RE

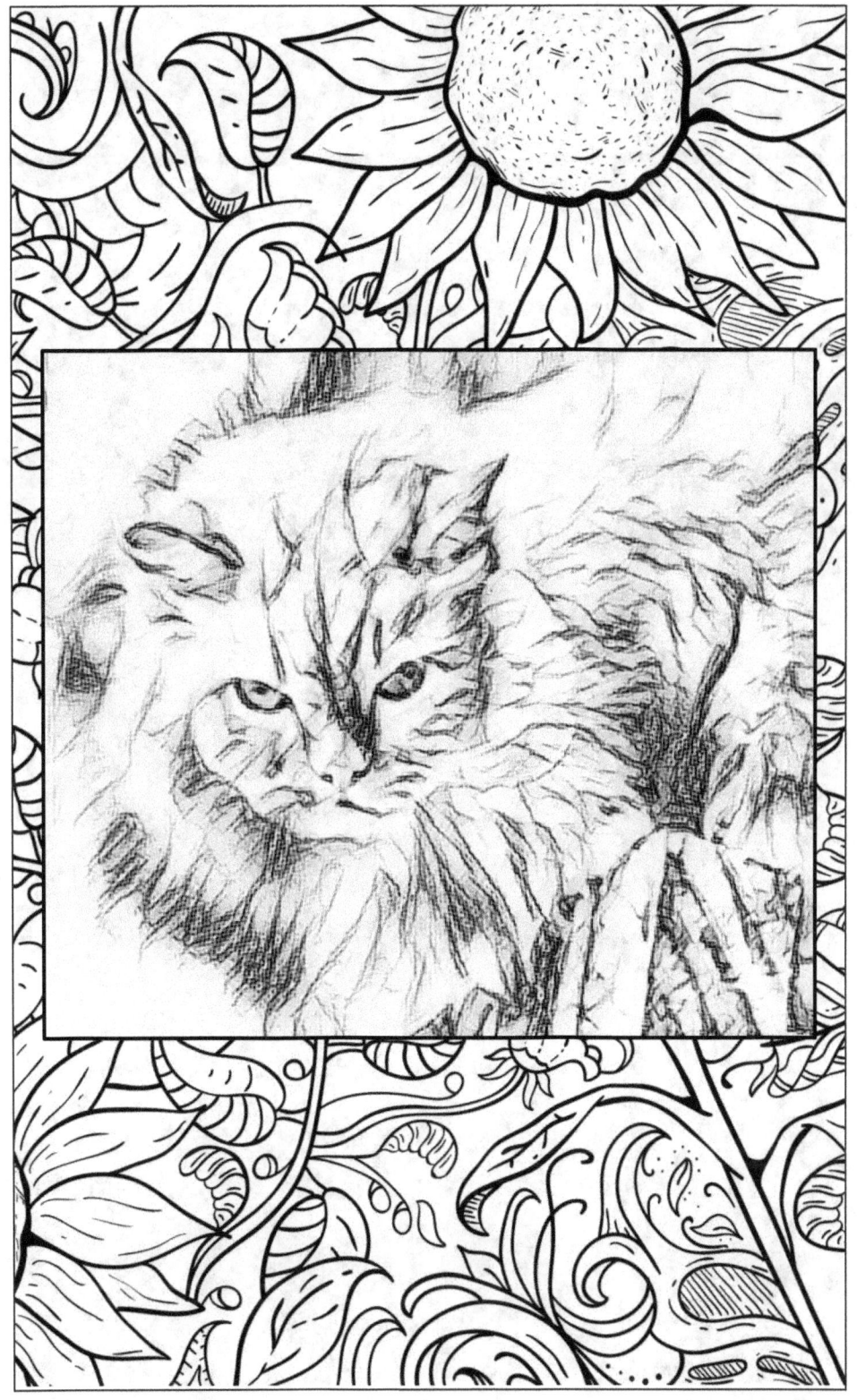

Today is
a good day
to have a
good day

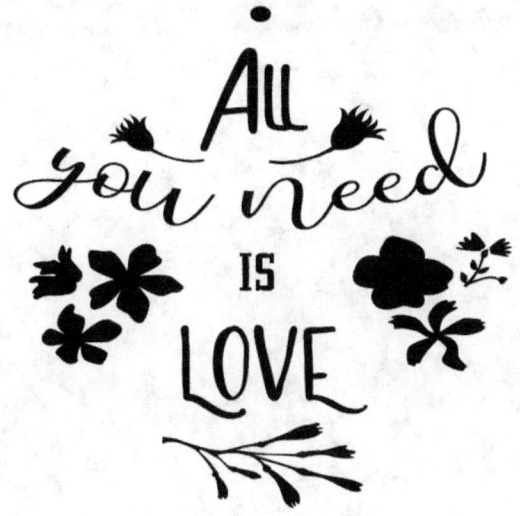

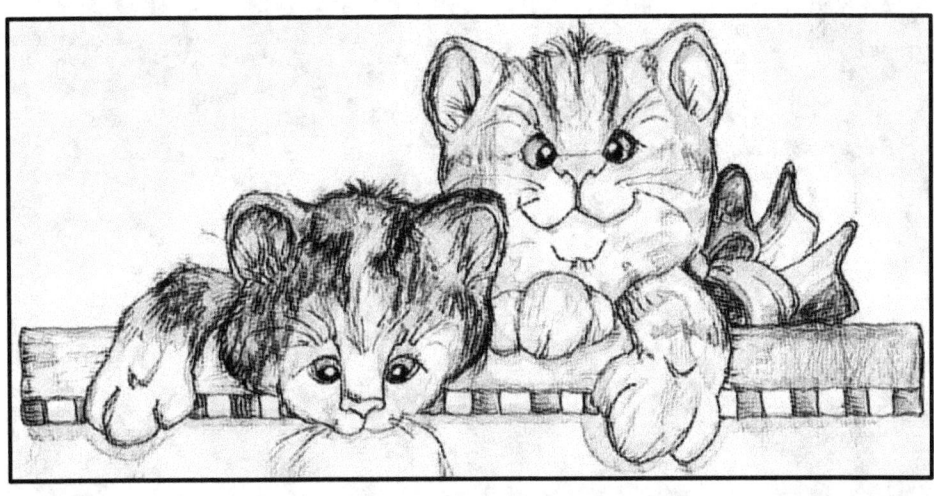

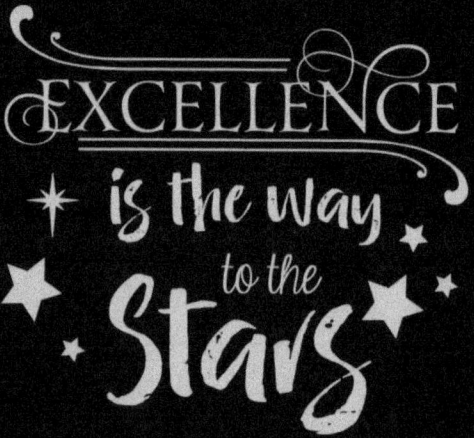

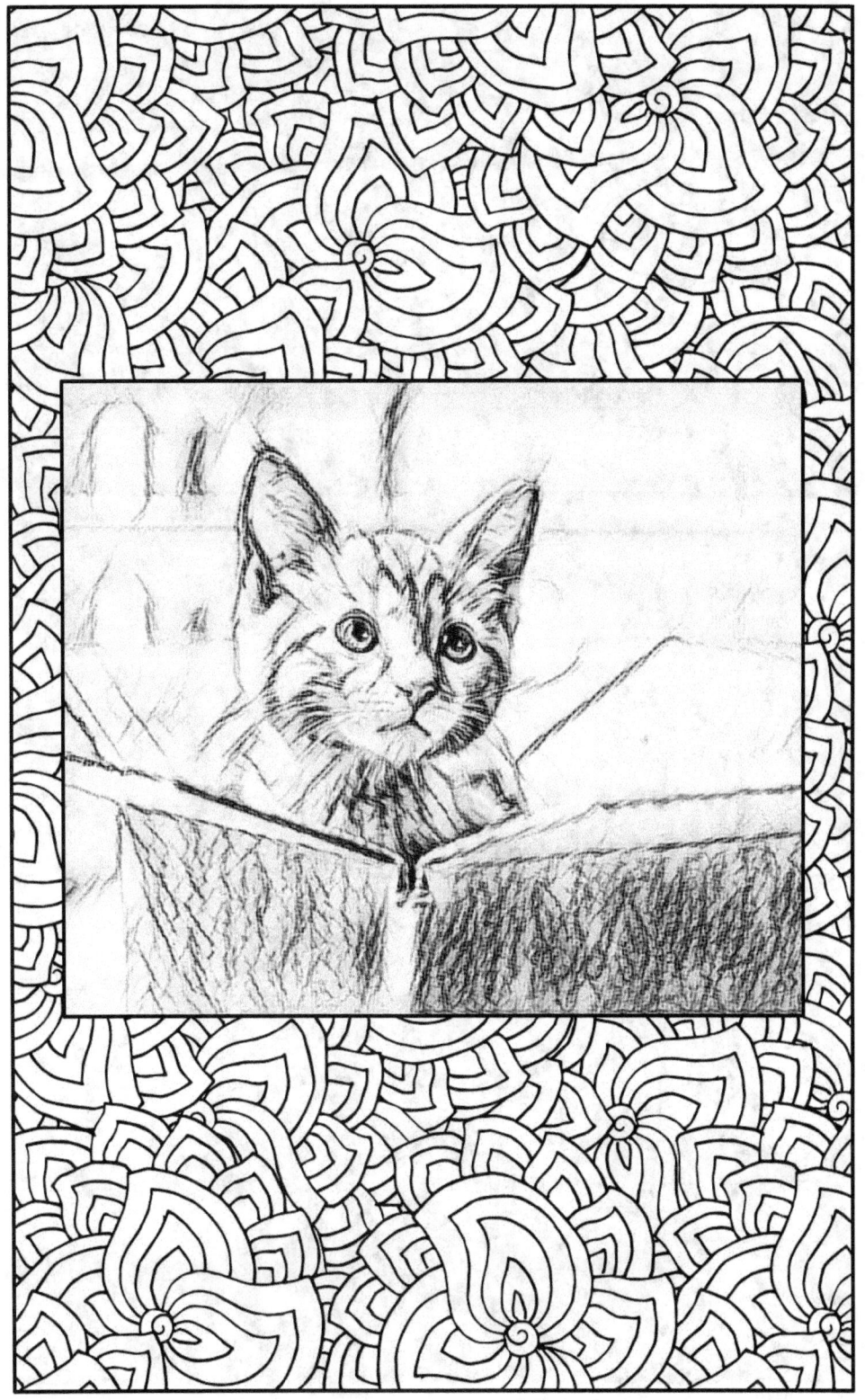

Stay Magical

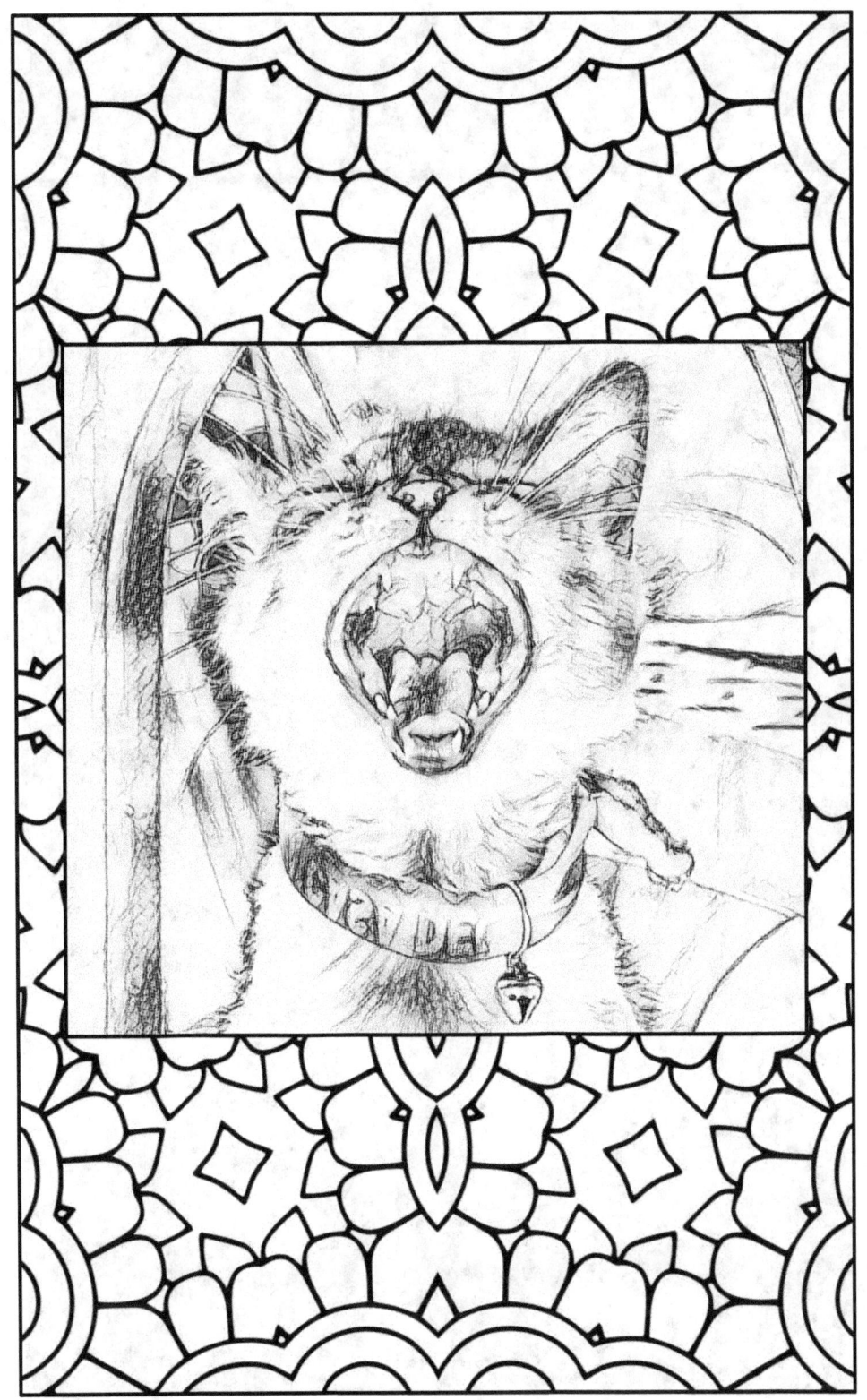

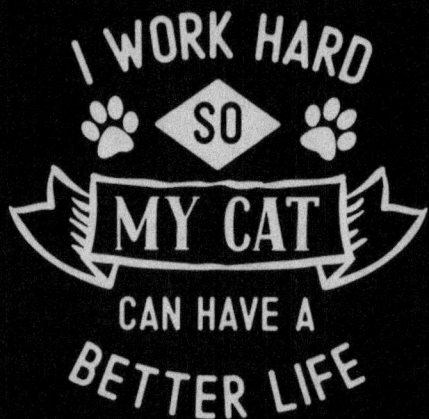

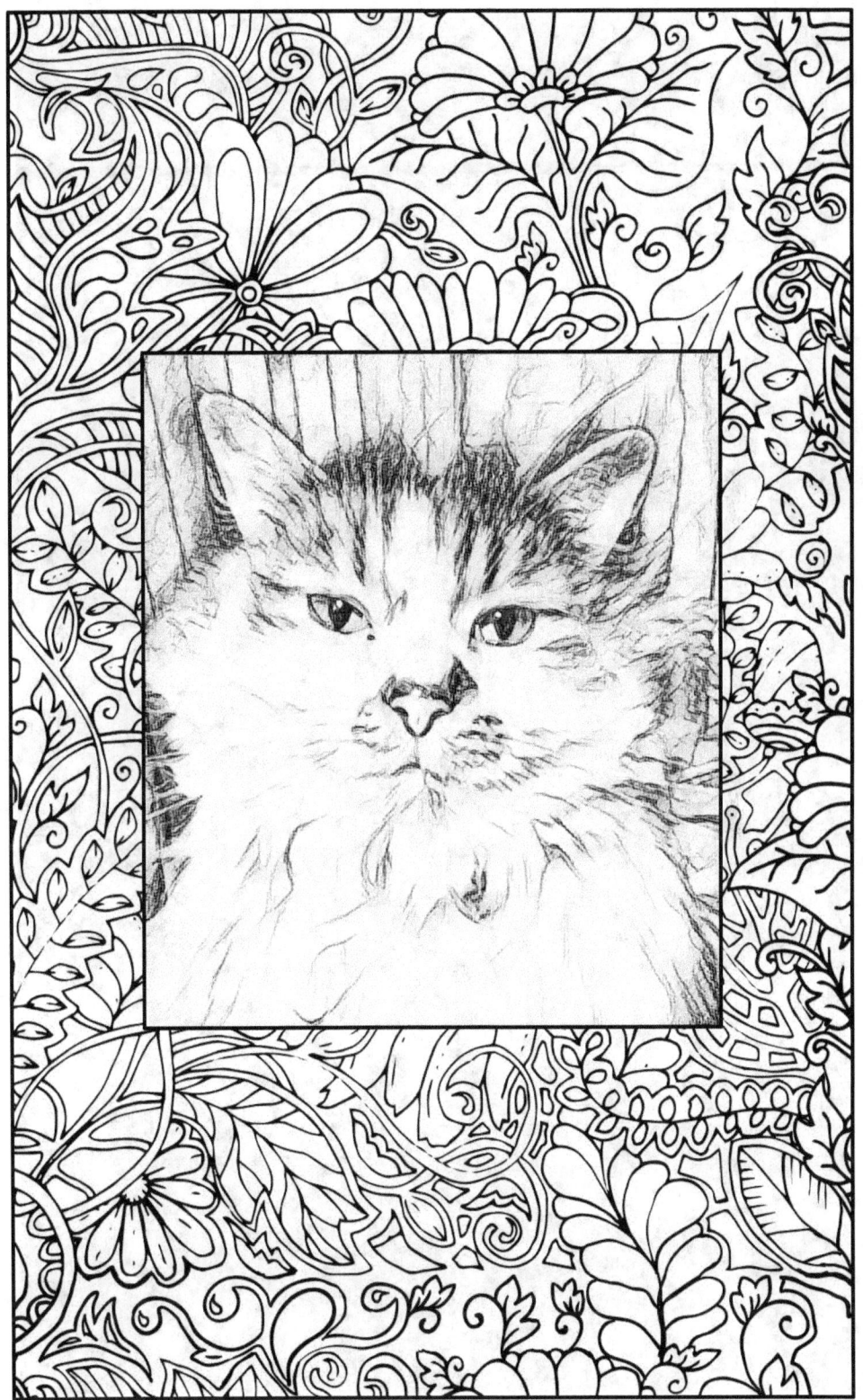

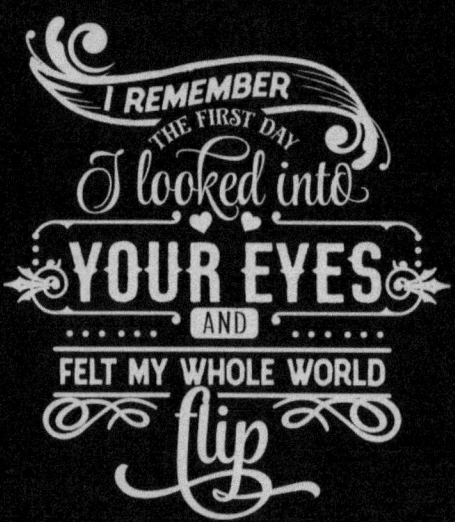

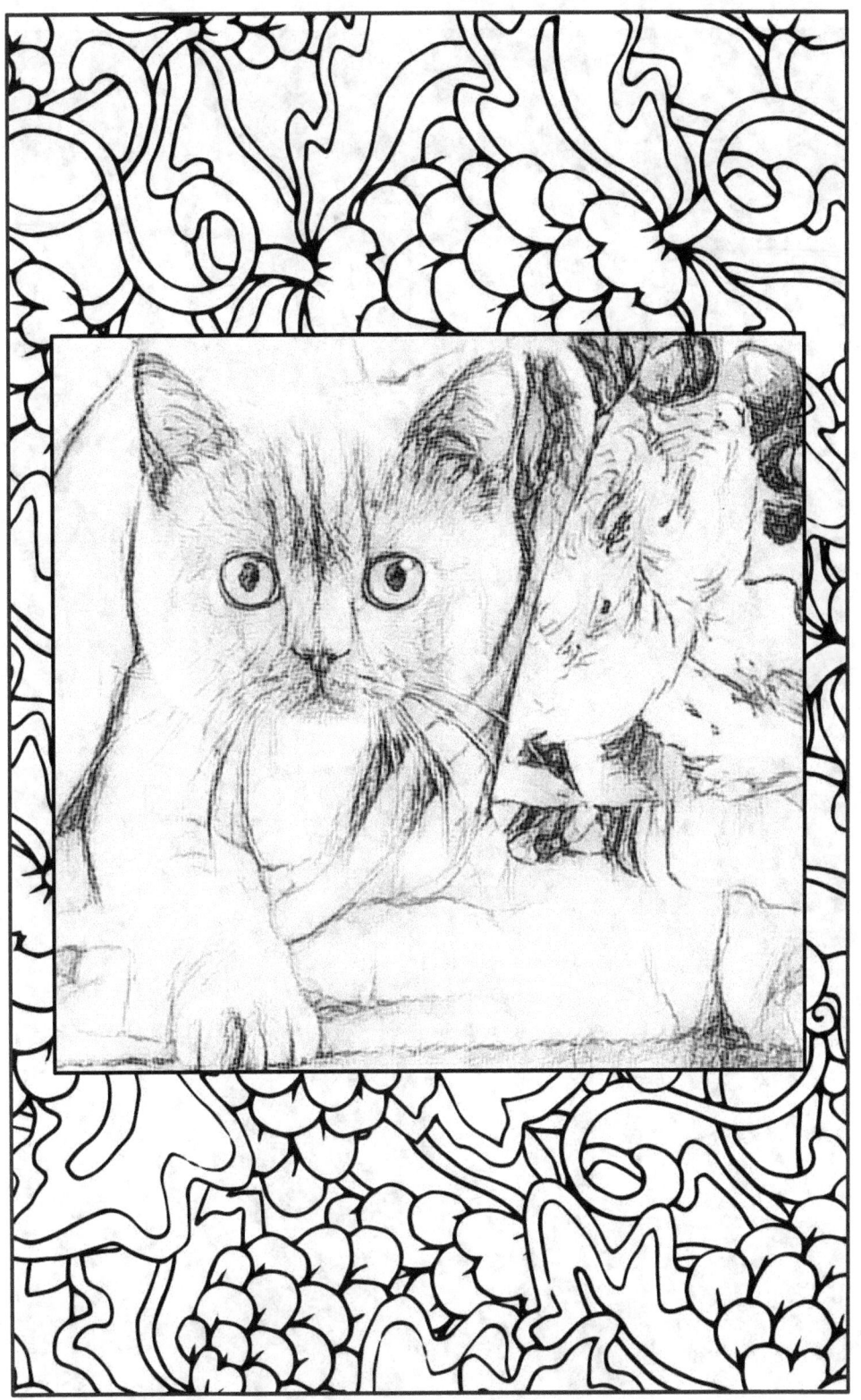

I AM
Enough
strong. beautiful. kind.
LOVED

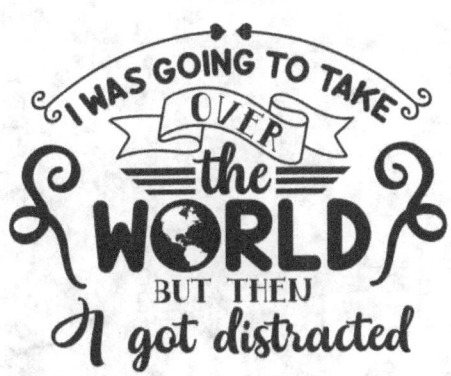

I WAS GOING TO TAKE OVER the WORLD BUT THEN I got distracted

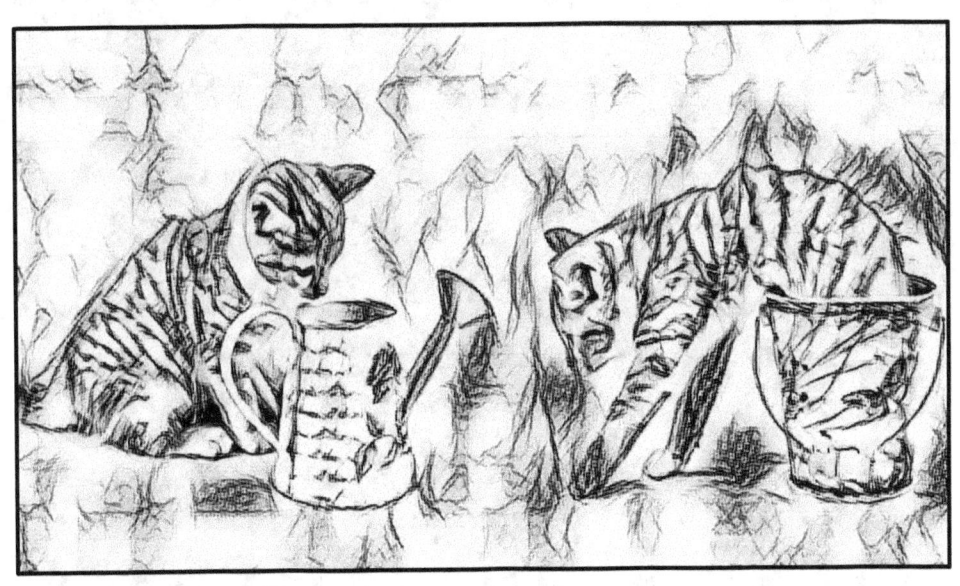

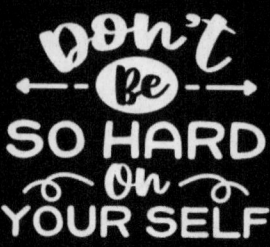

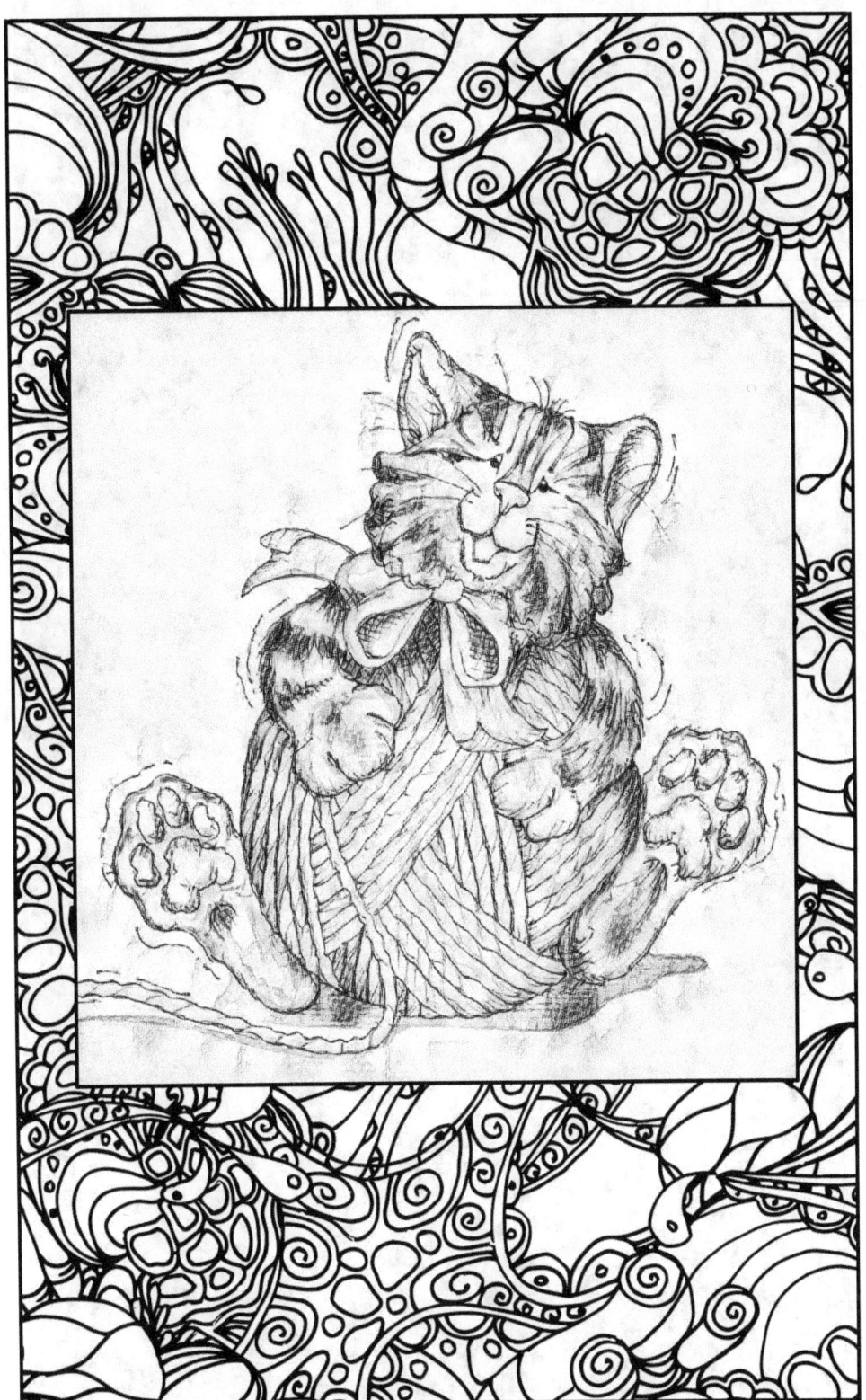

YOU CAN'T BUY
→LOVE→
♥ BUT YOU CAN ♥
RESCUE IT

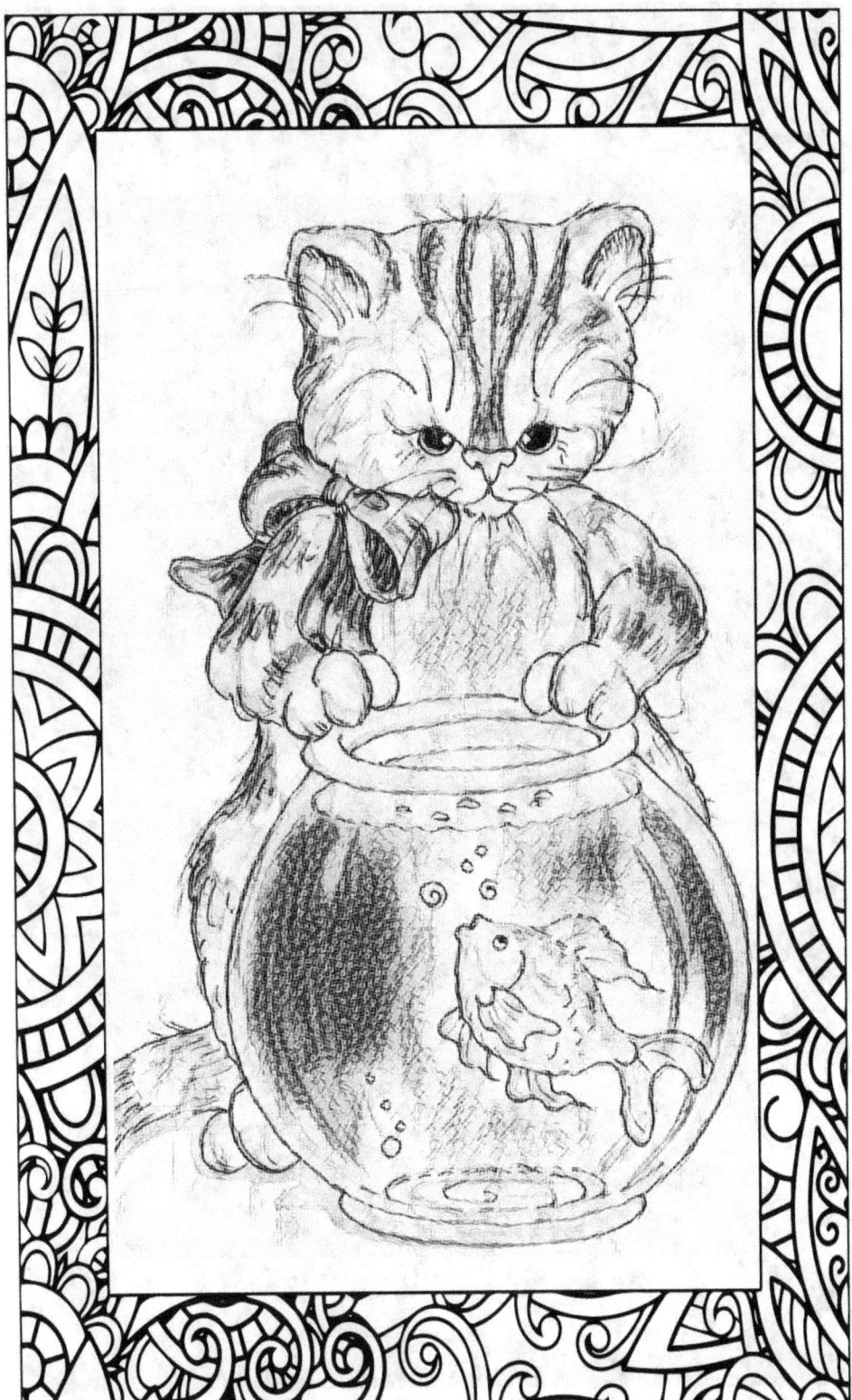

I JUST WANT TO BE A Stay AT Home CAT MOM

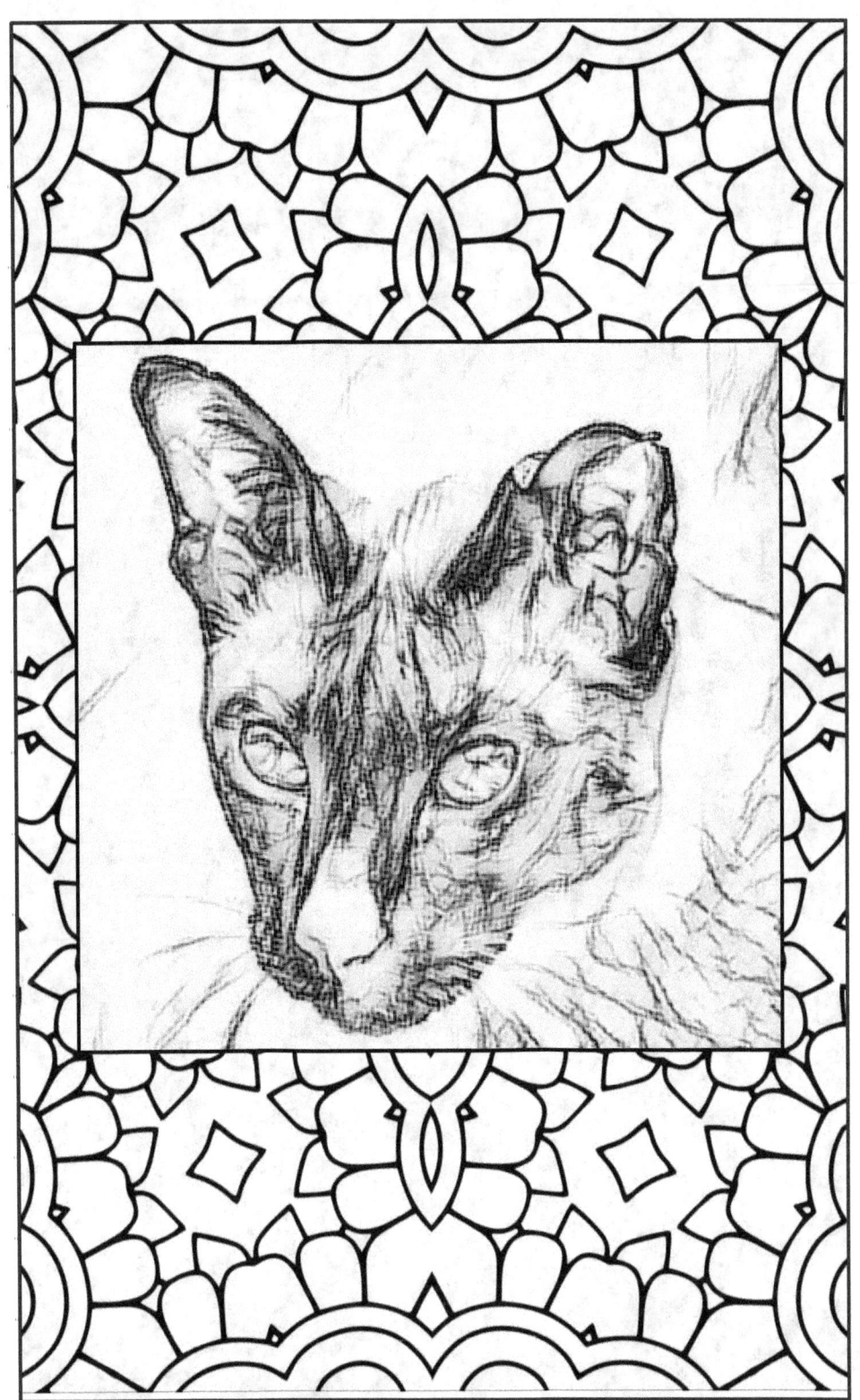

MY WORRIES
are few
BECAUSE MY
Blessings
ARE MANY

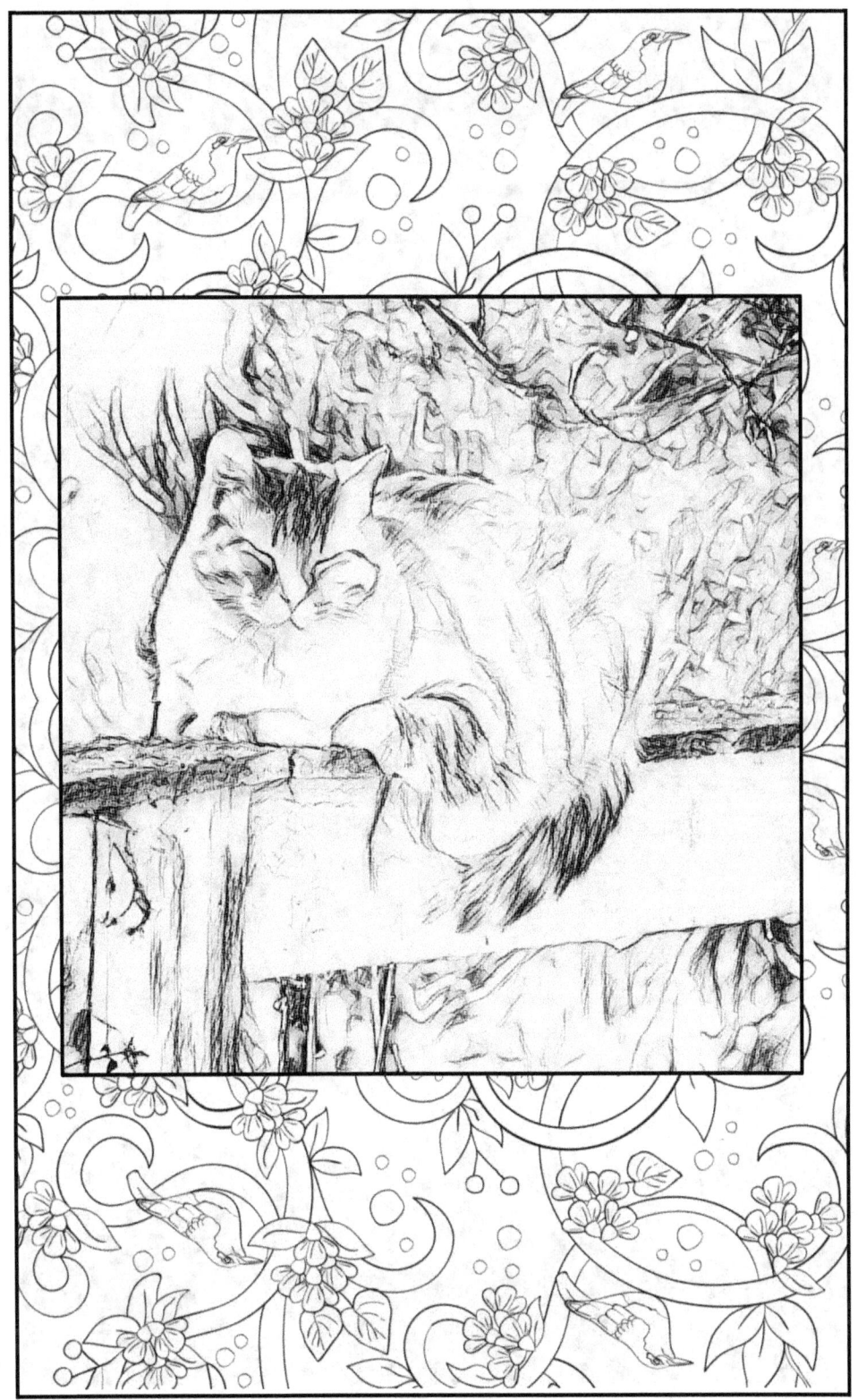

Be The
Reason
Someone
SMILES☺

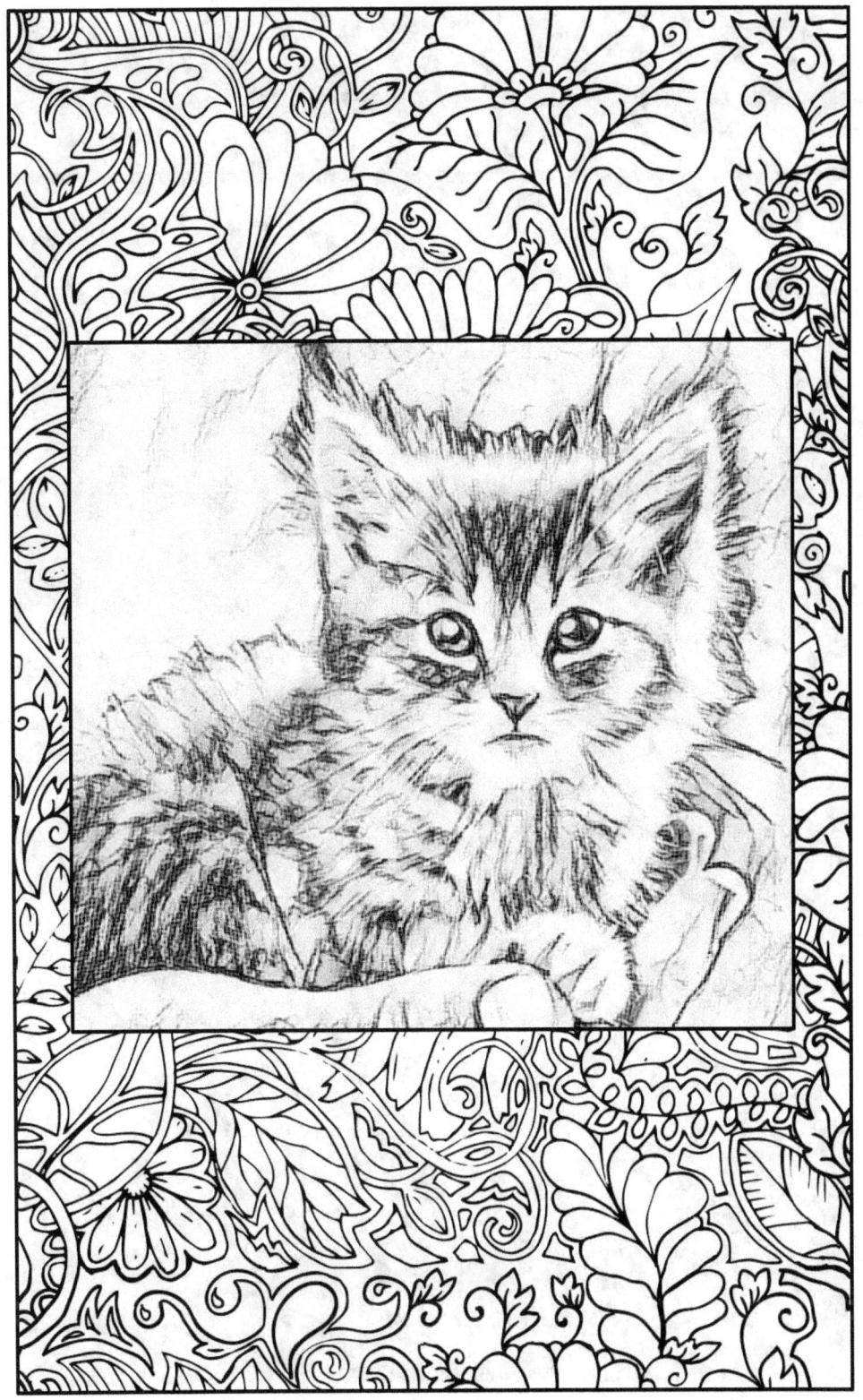

Plant
Dreams
pull
Weeds &
grow a
Happy Life

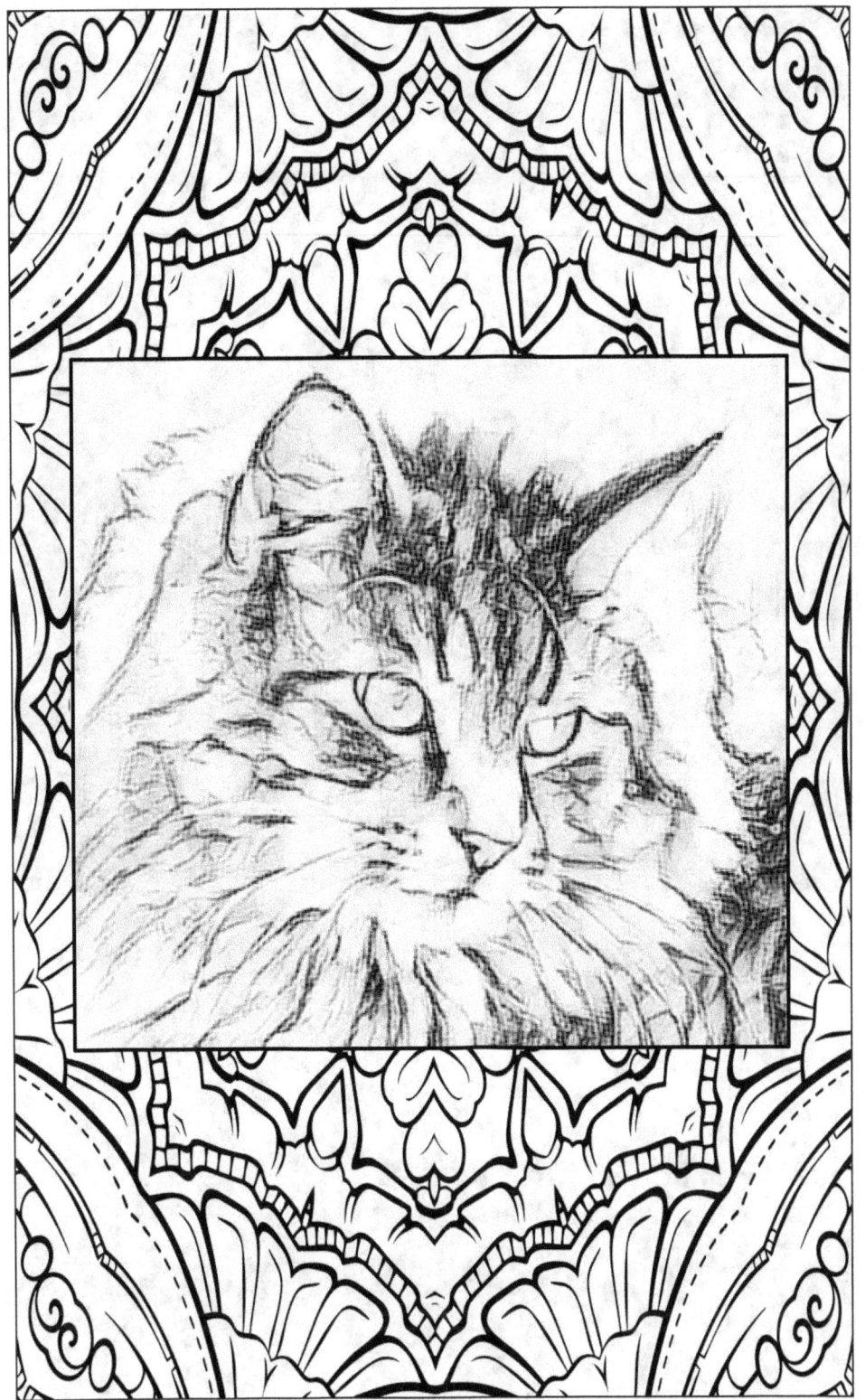

SEASON
EVERYTHING·
· WITH ·
Love

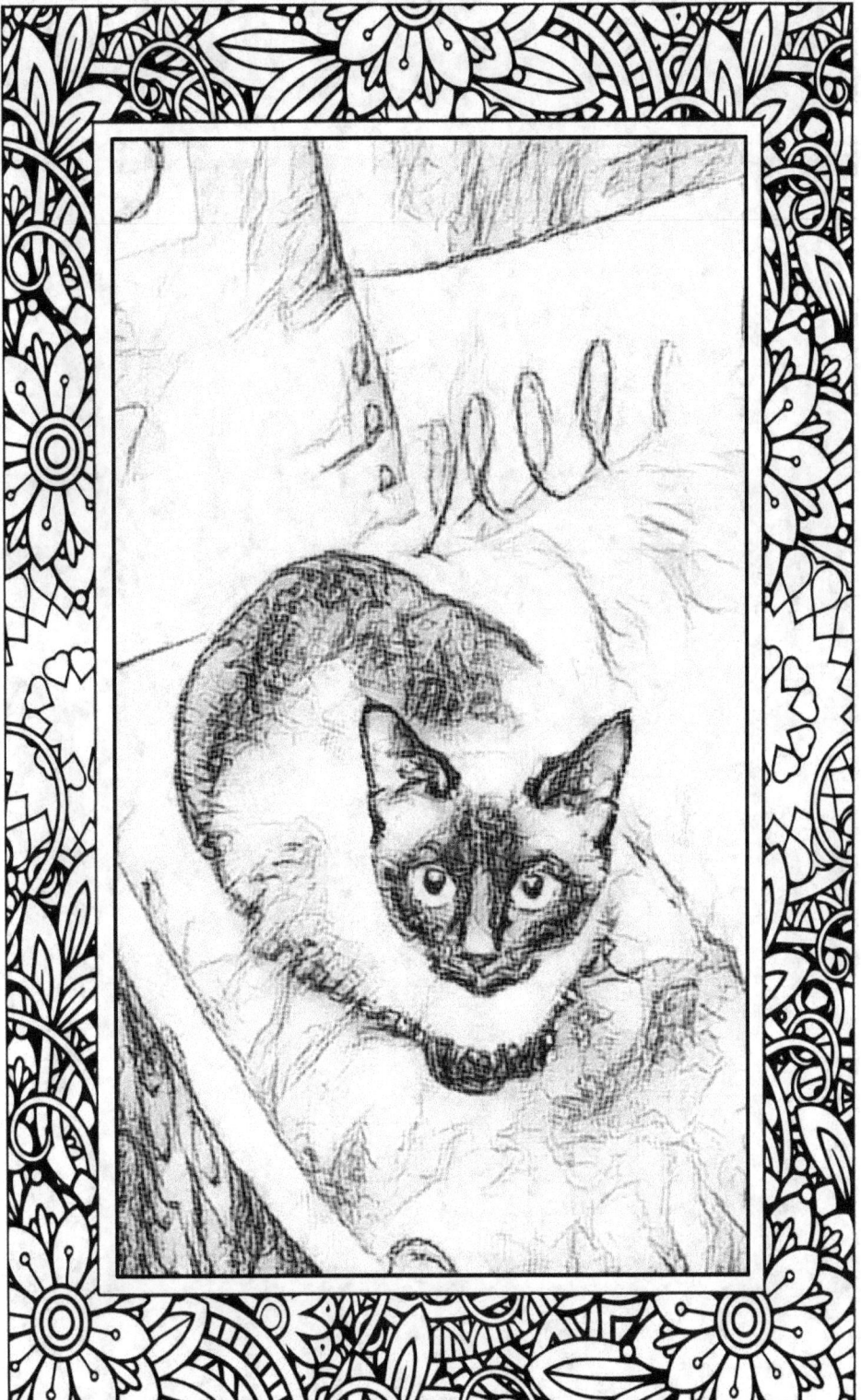

Be
yOURSELF
Everyone
ELSE IS
Taken

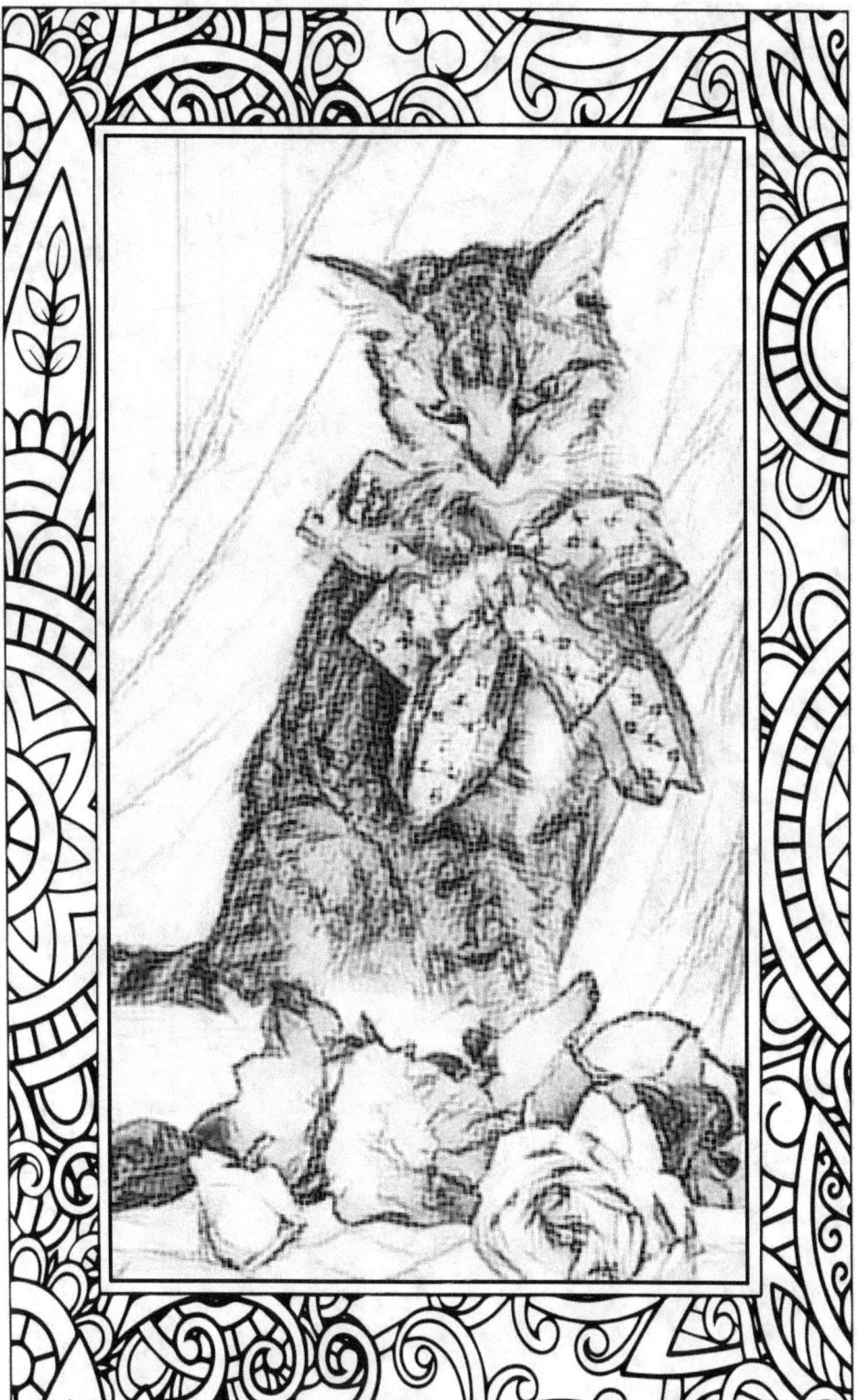

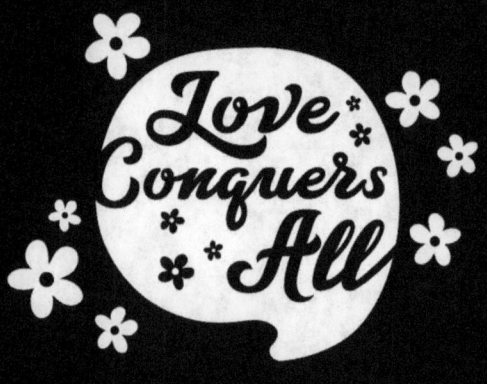

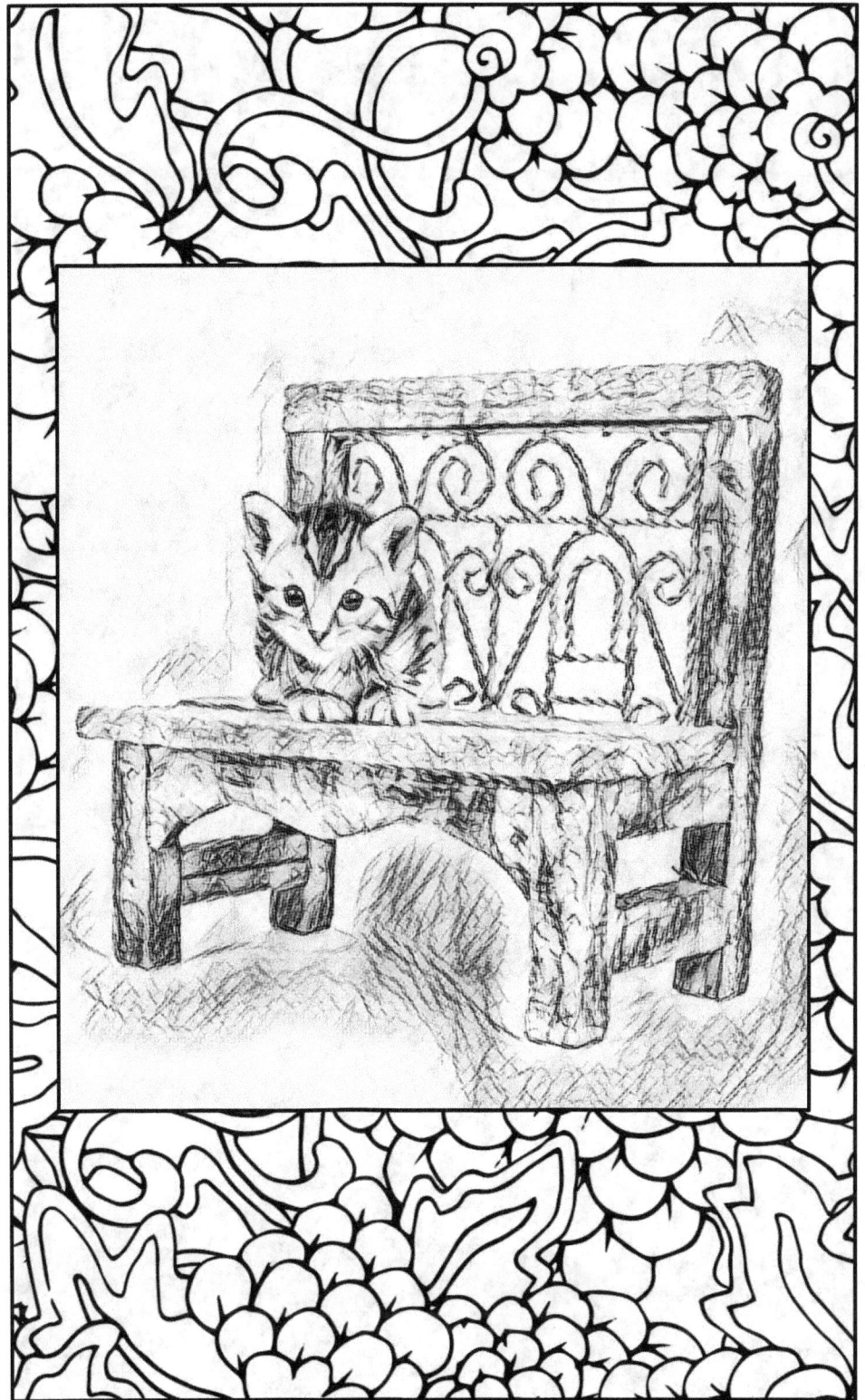

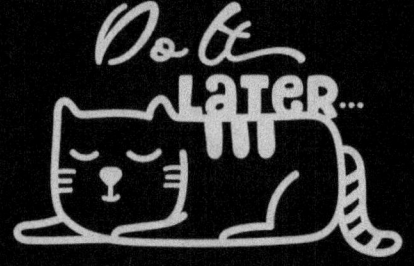

DON'T GIVE UP ON *YOUR* dreams KEEP SLEEPING

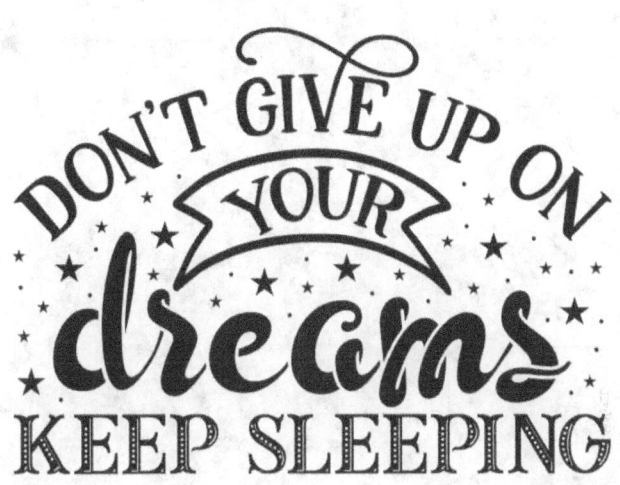

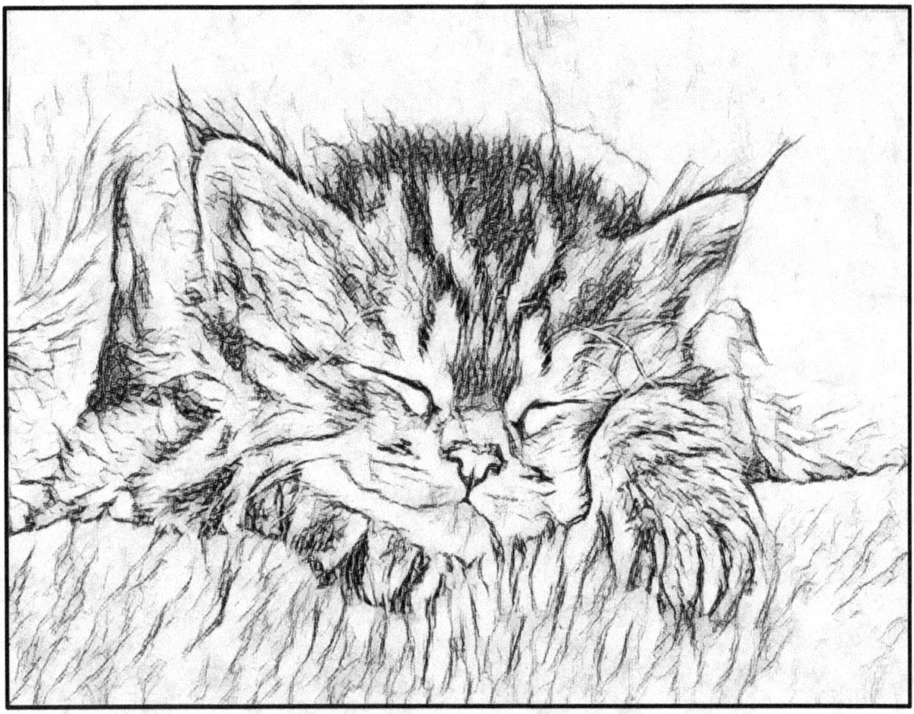

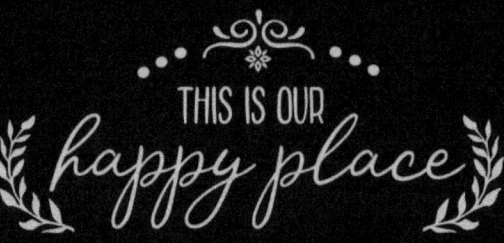

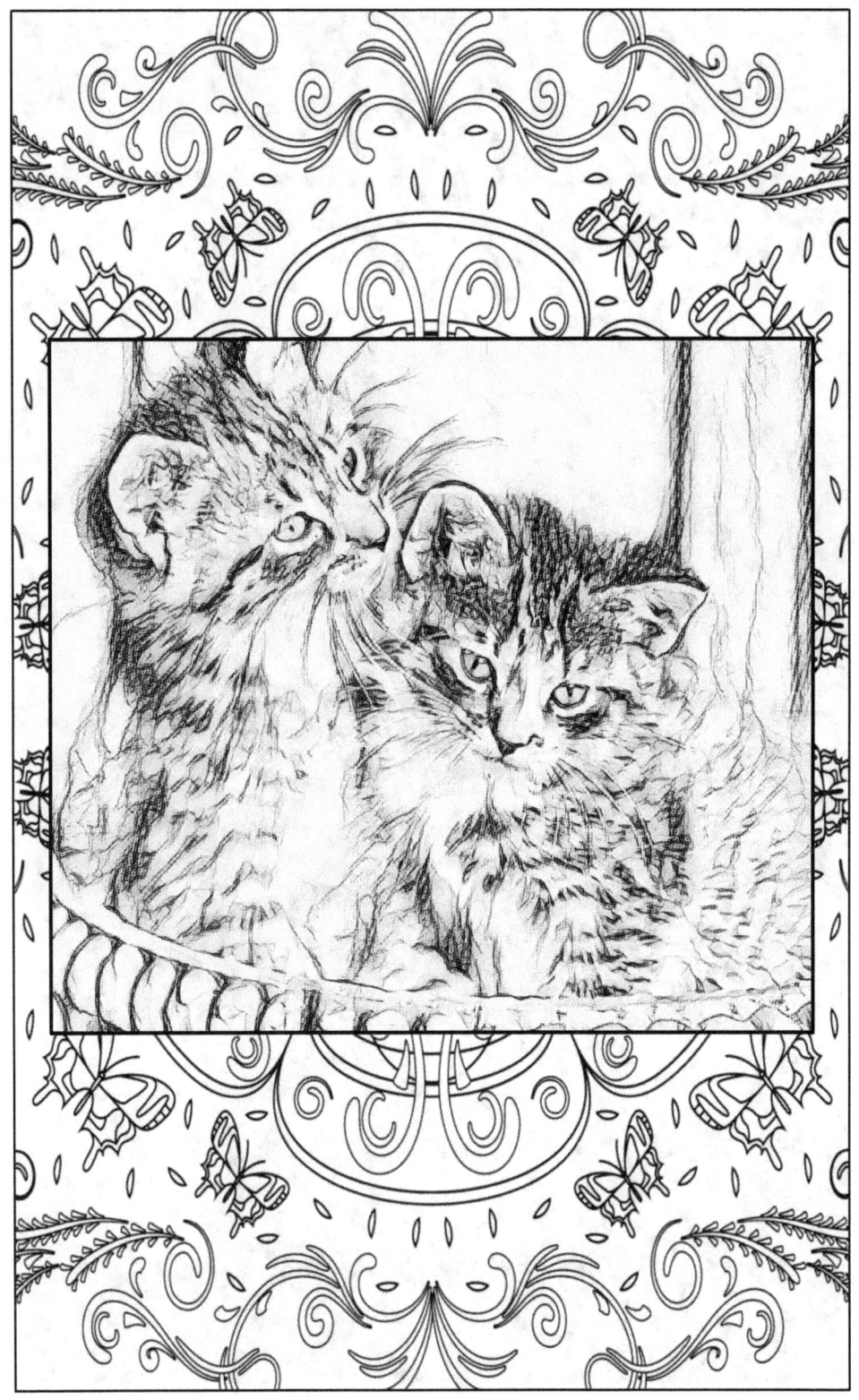

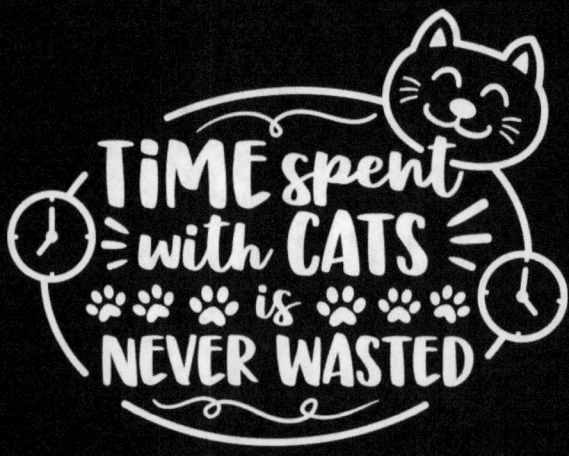

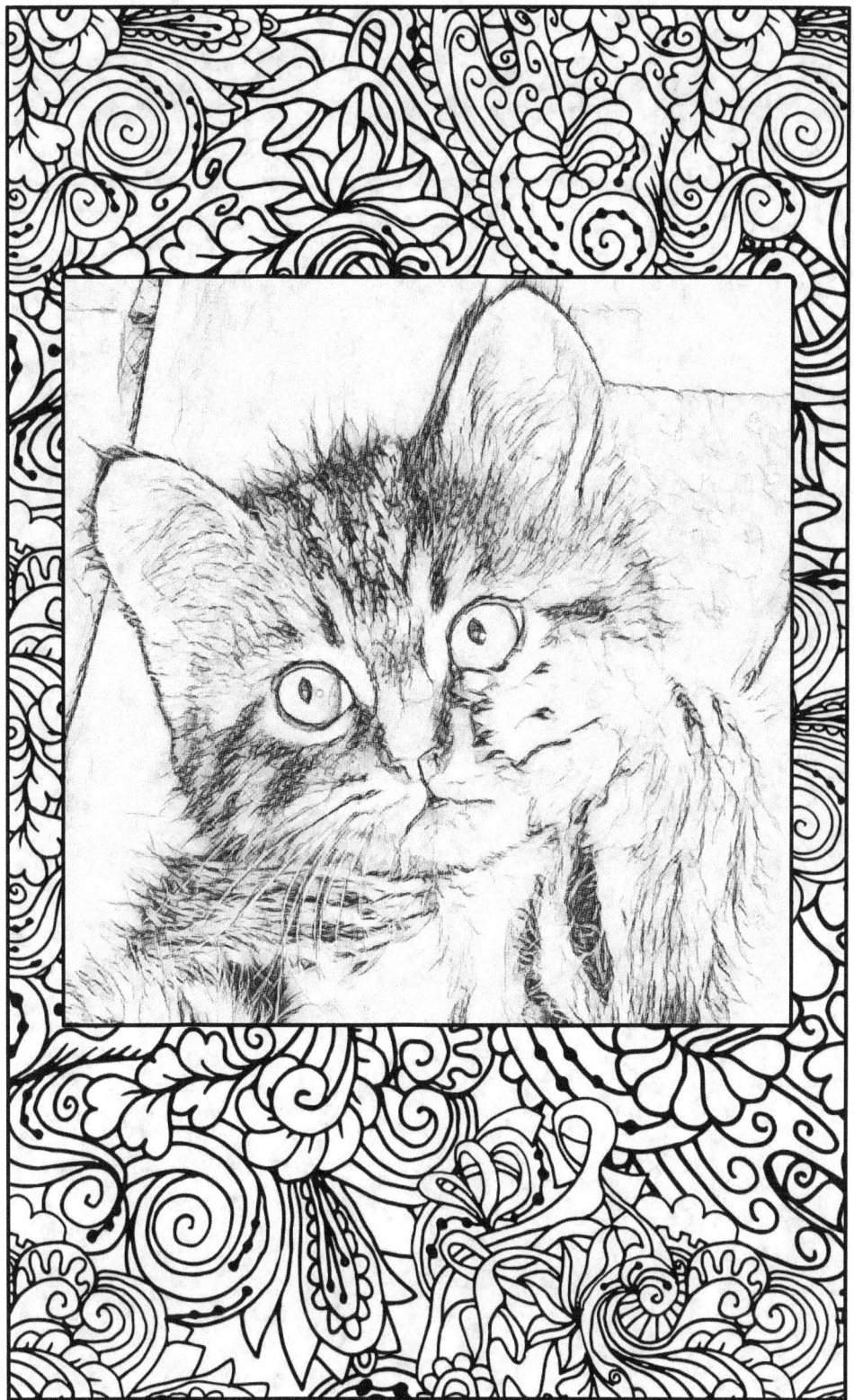

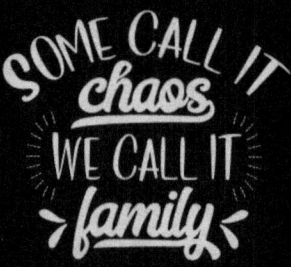

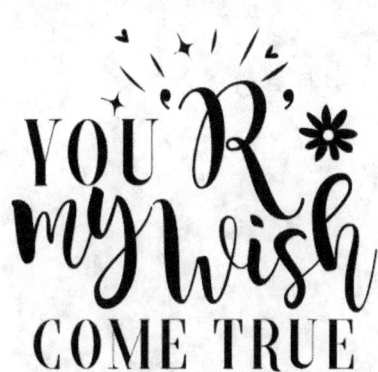

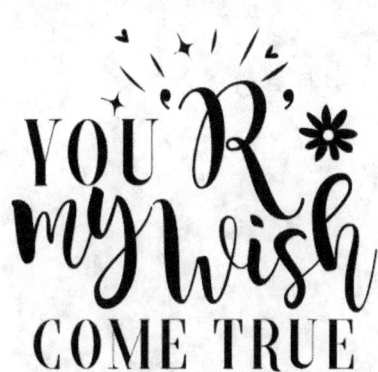

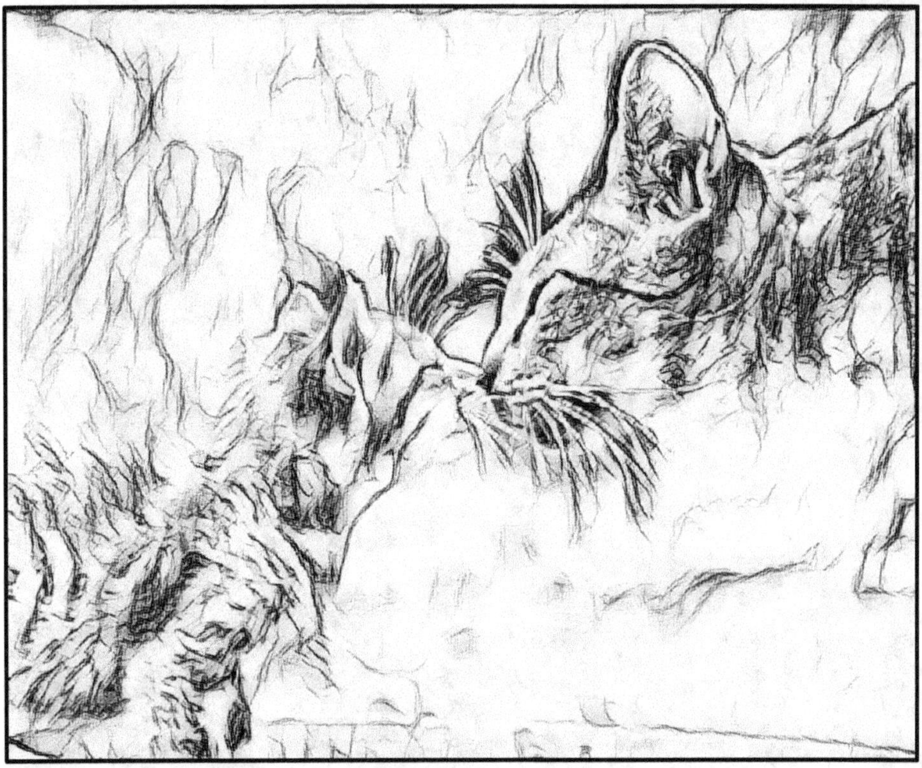

I WISH
NOTHING
❀ but ❀
THE BEST
FOR YOU

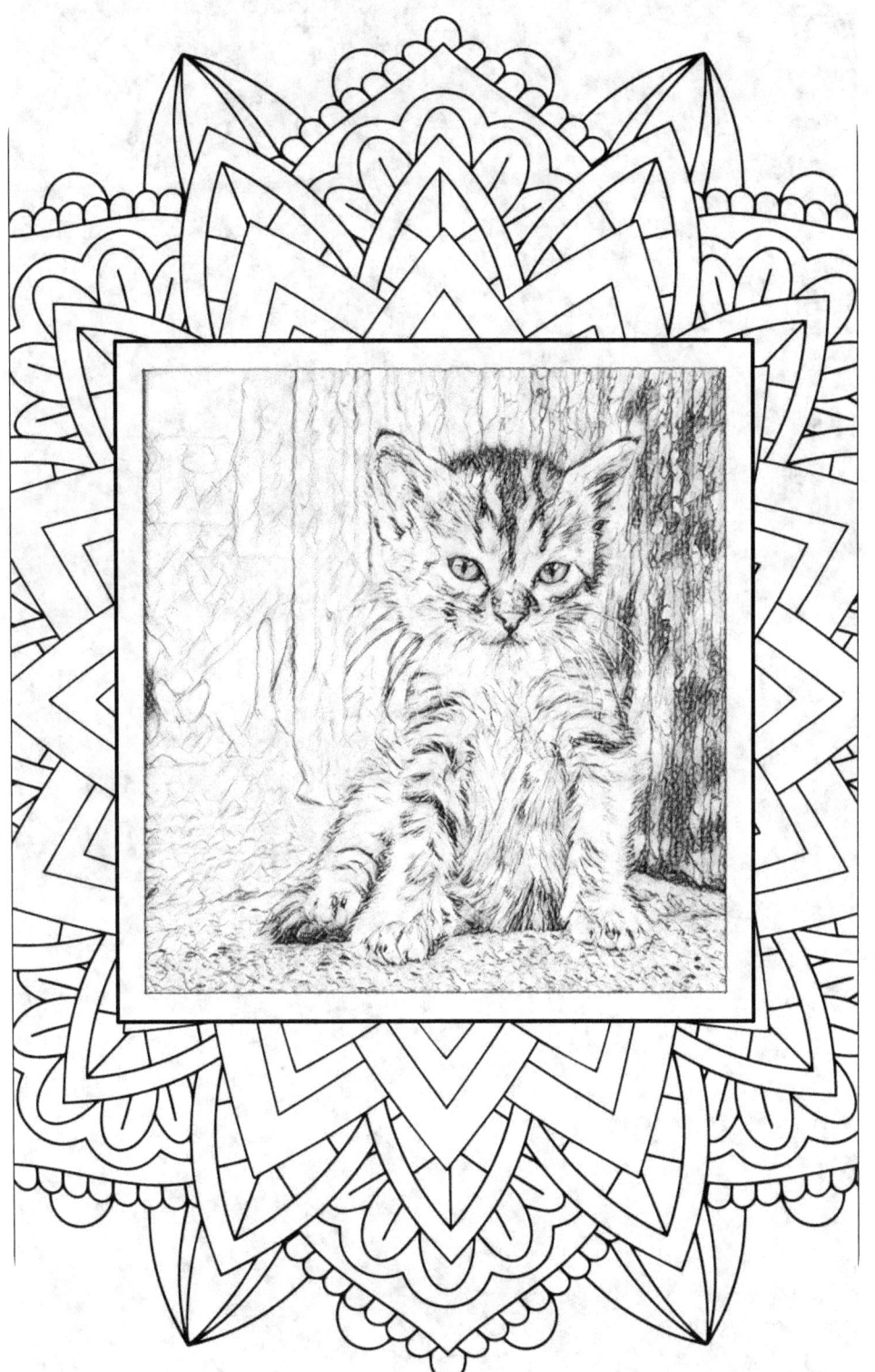

Cats Books & Coffee

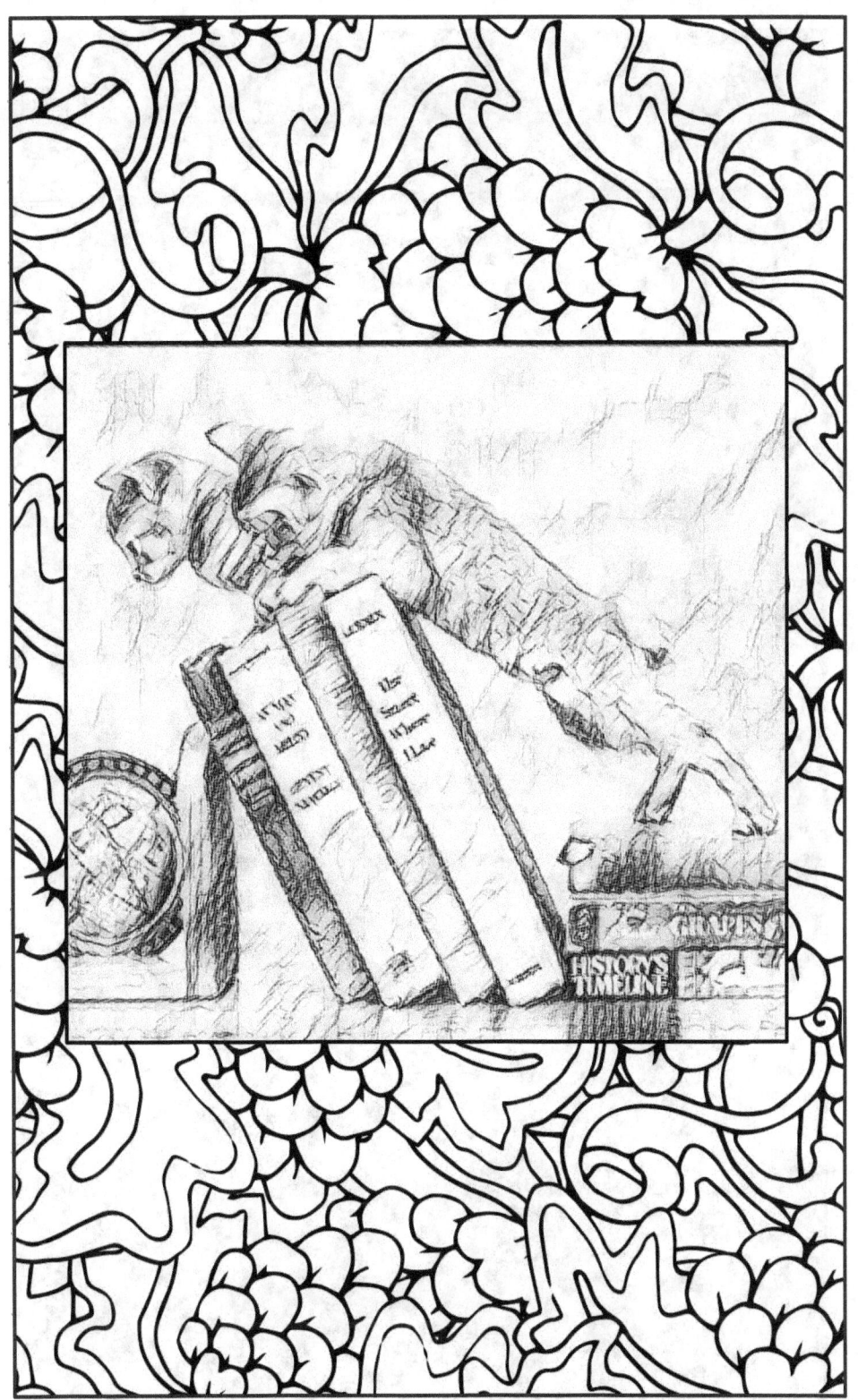

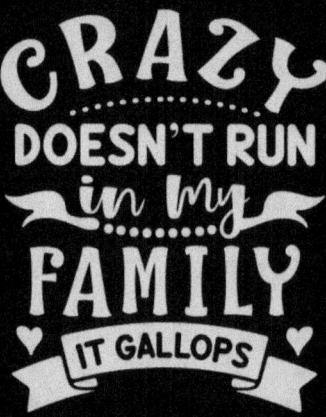

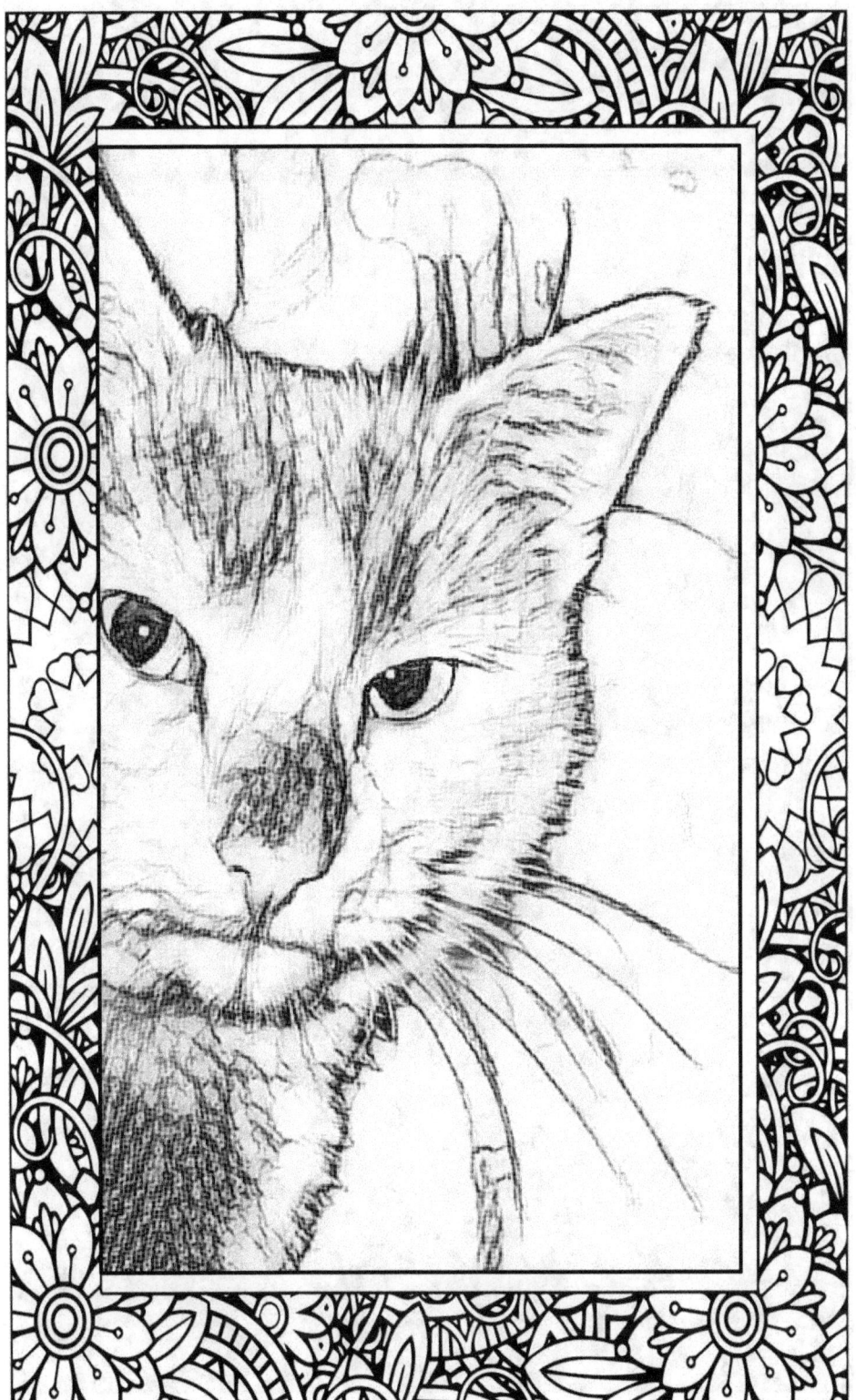

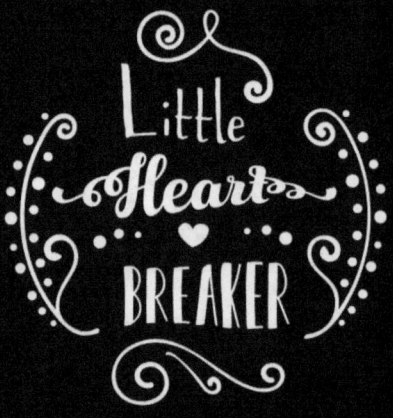

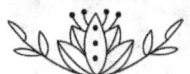

DO ALL THINGS WITH

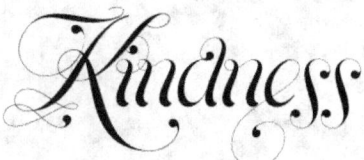

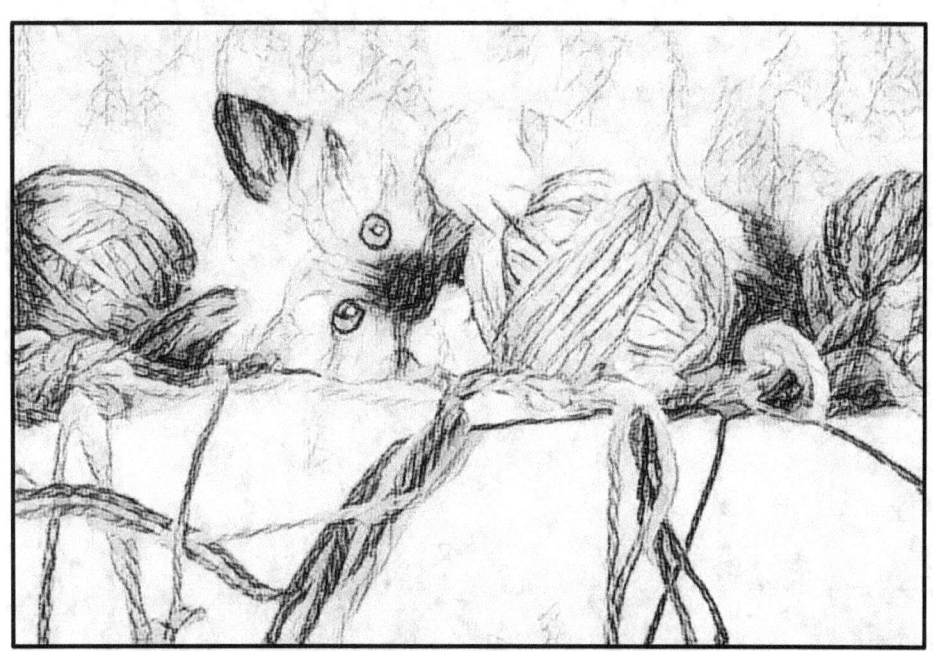

Family
IS
forever

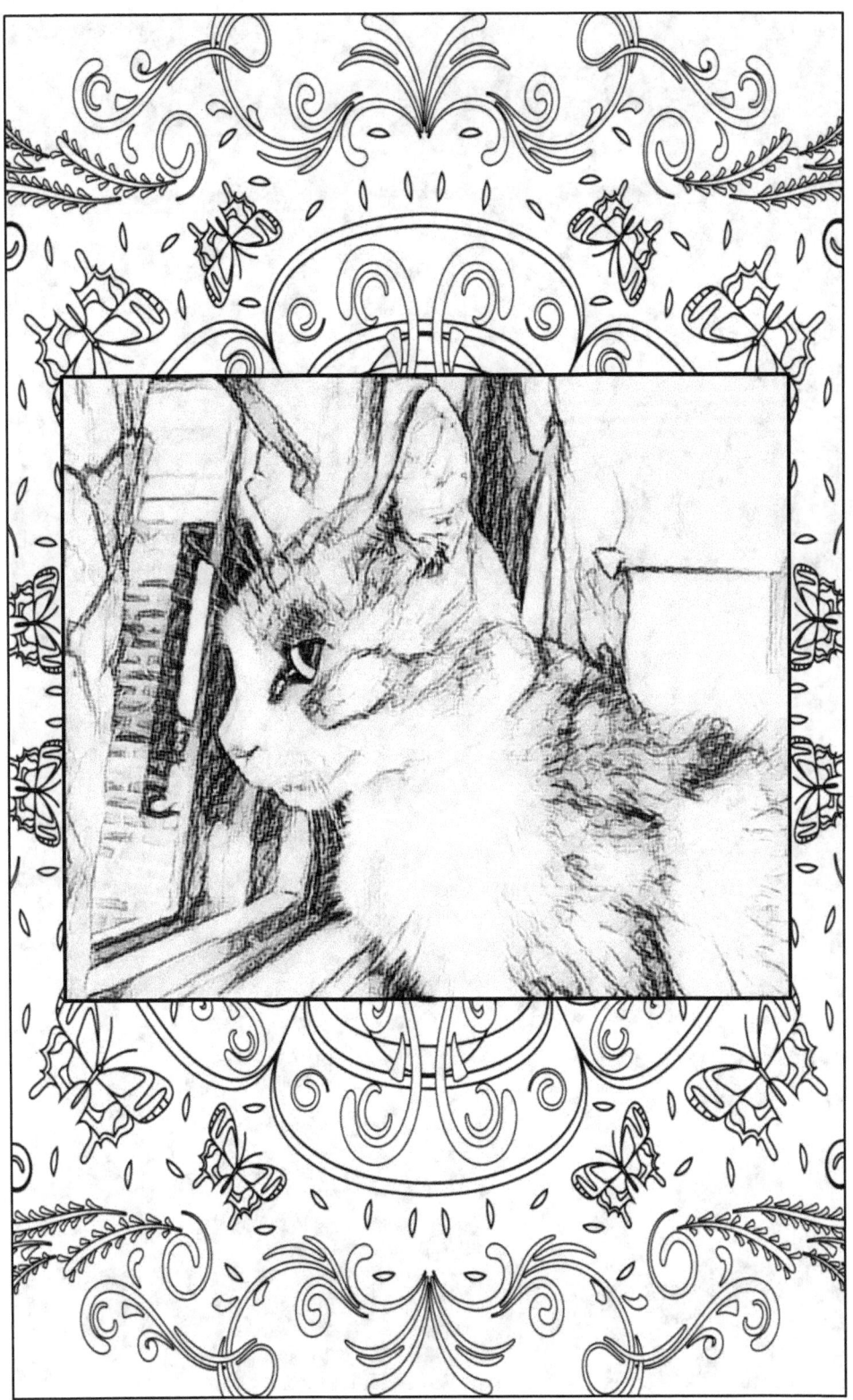

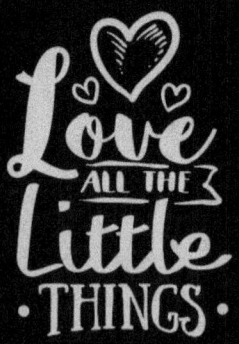

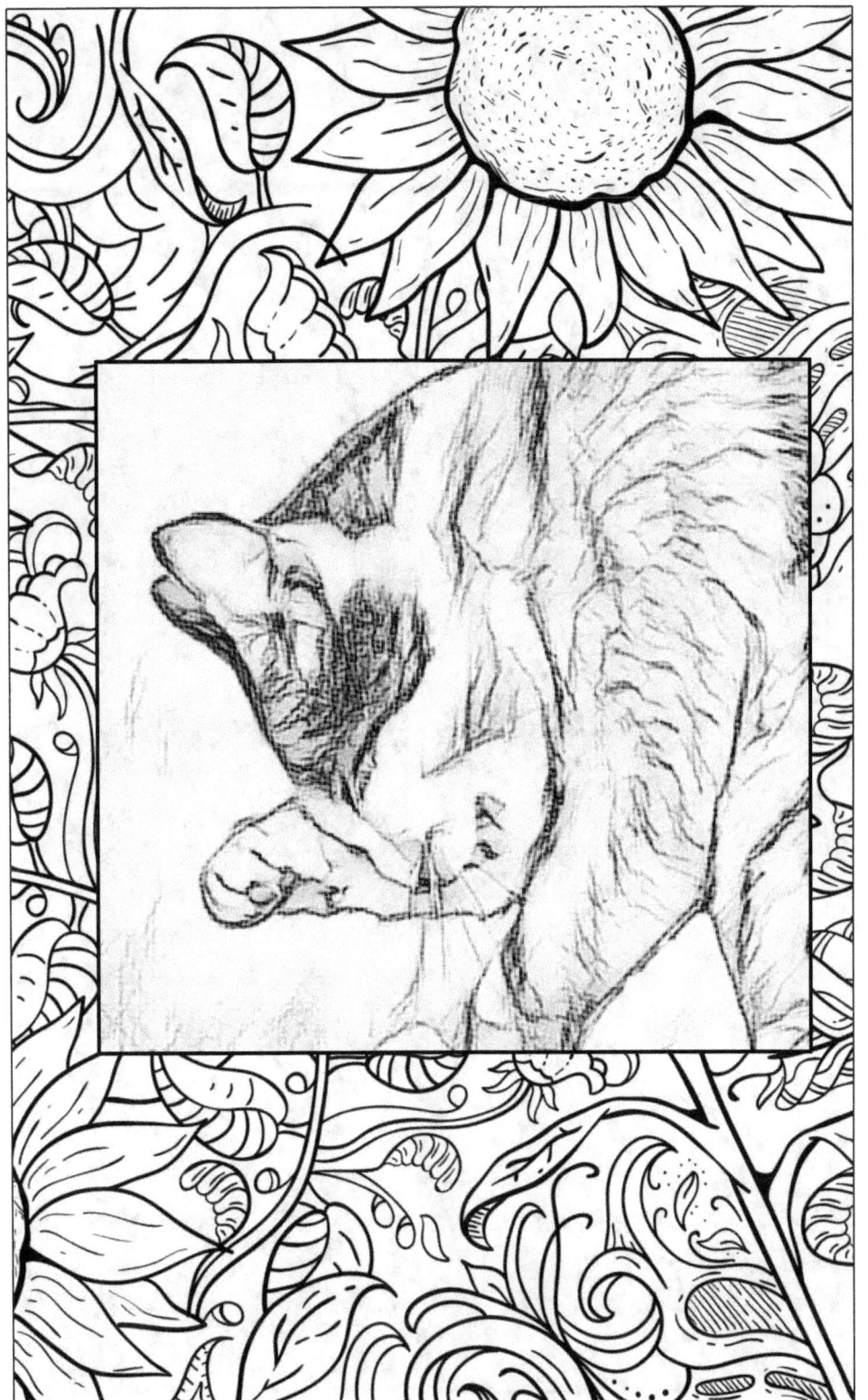

STOP
WISHING
Start..!
..doing

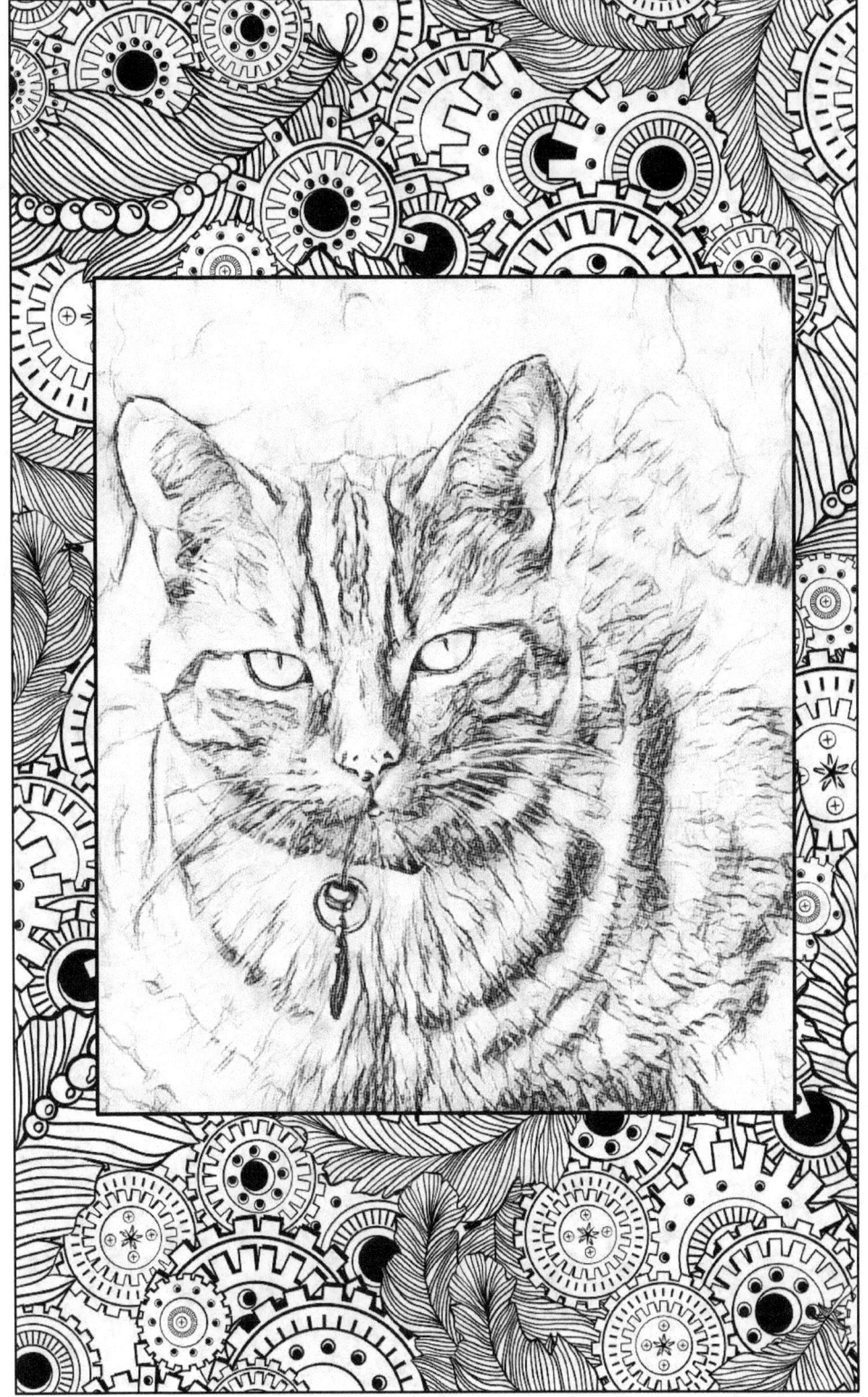

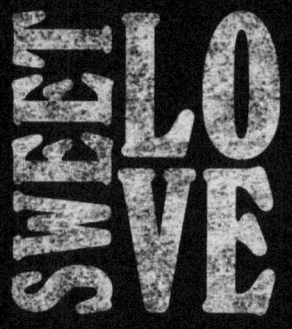

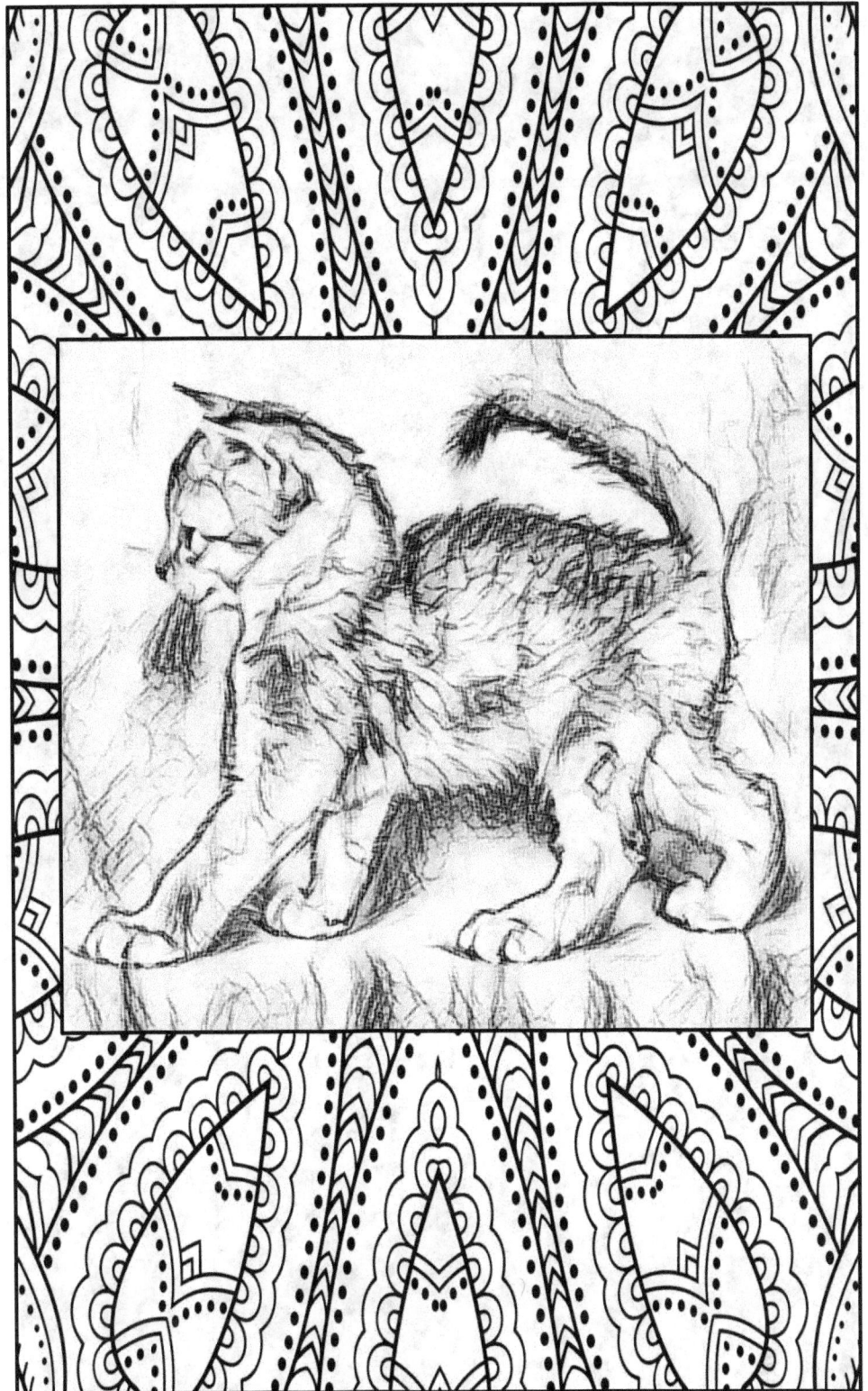

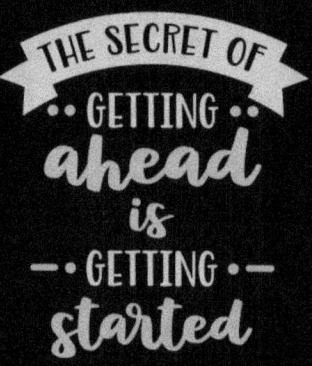

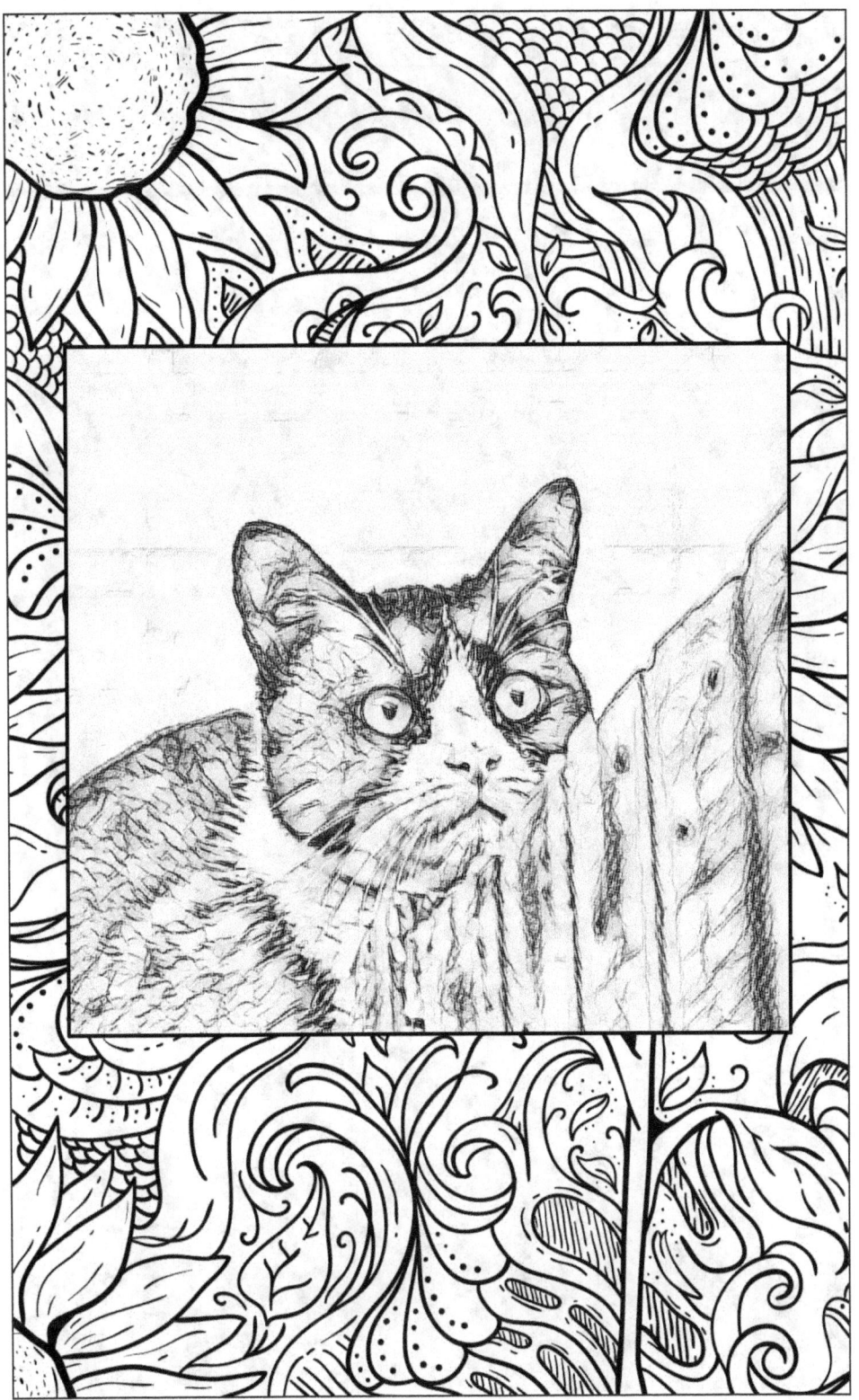

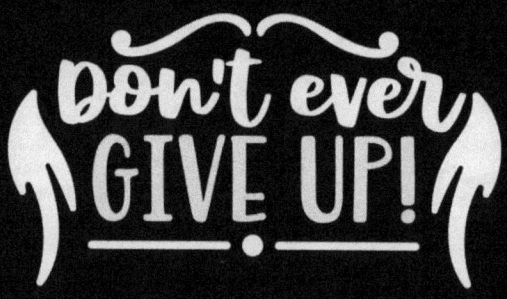

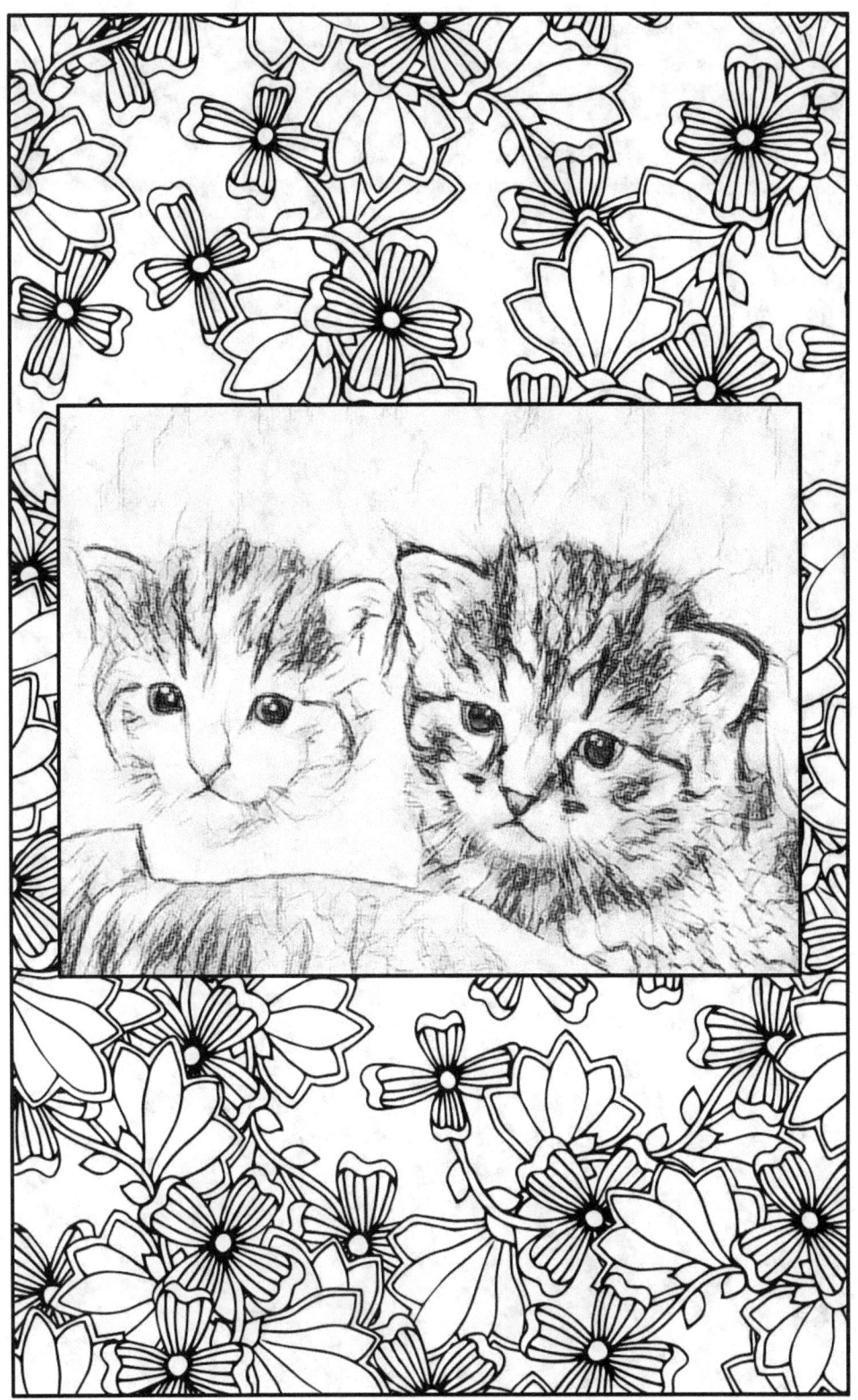

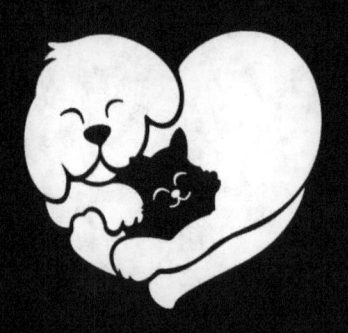

A lifetime fan of Diary & Journal creation for her own writing and embellishing, Helene Malmsio has compiled a collection of Diaries, Journals and Bullet dot grid Planners in paperback soft cover books for your pleasure

"When you use one of my Journals I want it to make you feel good. Knowing you can use these as a creative tool to craft a better life for yourself and your loved ones, is my inspiration – ENJOY!"

Other online resources from **Helene Malmsio** and **Strategic Publications**:

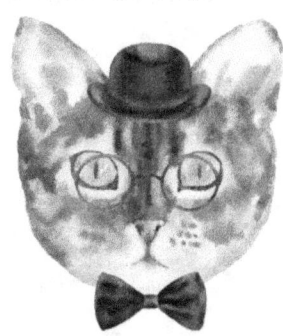

www.HeleneMalmsio.com
www.DiscoveryHub.net
www.PLRhub.net
www.ColourMeKind.com
www.Amazon.com/author/Strategic
www.lulu.com/spotlight/helenemalmsio

Thank you for your purchase of this book, as the bulk of the sales proceeds are used to help fund animal welfare organizations around the world, so you are helping to be the solution to a better kinder world when you buy from these resources.

And if you enjoyed this book, I would truly appreciate a simple comment in the book review section in the online sales page you ordered this book from.

"Be the change you wish to see in the world."
- Mahatma Gandhi

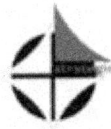

Strategic Services
Established in 1987